CABIN
STYLE

CABIN STYLE

CHASE REYNOLDS EWALD
Photographs by **AUDREY HALL**

GIBBS SMITH
TO ENRICH AND INSPIRE HUMANKIND

For Deb, who so generously shares her horses, her dogs, and her Rocky Mountain home.

—CRE

To my sister, Patty, in her loving memory.

—AH

First Edition
23 22 21 20 19   5 4 3 2 1

Text © 2019 Chase Reynolds Ewald
Photographs © 2019 Audrey Hall

Published by
Gibbs Smith
P.O. Box 667
Layton, Utah 84041

1.800.835.4993 orders
www.gibbs-smith.com

Designed by Sheryl Dickert
Page production by Renee Bond & Virginia Snow
Printed and bound in China

Gibbs Smith books are printed on either recycled, 100% post-consumer waste, FSC-certified papers or on paper produced from sustainable PEFC-certified forest/controlled wood source.
Learn more at www.pefc.org.

Library of Congress Cataloging-in-Publication Data

Names: Ewald, Chase Reynolds, 1963- author. | Hall, Audrey, photographer.
Title: Cabin style / Chase Reynolds Ewald ; photographs by Audrey Hall.
Description: First edition. | Layton, Utah : Gibbs Smith, [2019]
Identifiers: LCCN 2018060846 | ISBN 9781423652465 (jacketless hardcover)
Subjects: LCSH: Log cabins—United States. | Vacation homes—United States. | Second homes—United States. | Decoration and ornament, Rustic—United States. | Architecture, Modern—21st century.
Classification: LCC NA8470 .E93 2019 | DDC 728.7/30973—dc23
LC record available at https://lccn.loc.gov/2018060846

CONTENTS

ACKNOWLEDGMENTS

Cabin Style, our fifth collaboration, represents the culmination of many miles on the road, many months in the making, and many hours in the design and polishing, all resting on many decades of sustained effort on the part of the architects, designers, builders, craftspeople, and artists whose work is showcased in these pages.

We so greatly appreciate the generous homeowners who, at inconvenience to themselves, allow us to feature their homes. They do it for the sake of the designers and builders so their work can be shared, as it so richly deserves.

We couldn't have done it without the unsung heroes working behind the scenes to make it all happen, particularly Becky Traucht from JLF Architects, Darcey Prichard from CLB Architects, Libby Delgado from Locati Architects, Deborah Monaghan from Envi Design, and a score of others who keep the wheels turning smoothly so the design luminaries are free to create their work. A huge thanks also to the caretakers, managers, and administrative assistants who provide access and coordinate schedules.

We greatly appreciate the magazine editors and art directors with whom we regularly work, including Darla Worden and Loneta Showell *at Mountain Living,* Christine Rogel and Dominique Fultz at *Western Art and Architecture,* Corinne Garcia and Geoff Hill at *Big Sky Journal,* Jennifer Kopf and Maribeth Jones at *Country Living,* and Ken Amorosano at *Cowgirl* for providing a forum for showcasing contemporary design in the most beautiful corners of America. Thanks to their efforts, one doesn't have to travel or own a country home to experience the extraordinary architecture and design being produced today.

The staff at Gibbs Smith has done a wonderful job with all our books, for which we are truly grateful. Our tireless and unflappable longtime editor Madge Baird answers emails at all hours of the night and weekends; she keeps pages moving through the process with efficiency, accuracy, professional expertise, and kindness. Book designers Sheryl Dickert, Renee Bond, and Virginia Brimhall Snow did justice to the beauty of the homes on the first go-round, while also accepting requests and late additions with grace. Thanks to the vision of firm founder Gibbs Smith—whose loss we all feel so profoundly and whose keen ear for a story launched so many books—the professionals at Gibbs Smith present our work in the best possible light.

We owe a huge debt of gratitude to the photo shoot team—Kristen Newbern, Alexander Simpson, Daniel Caudill, Ezra Olson, Jeni Fleming, Mary Grace, Hollie Wood, Liz Strong, and Amanda Jordan—for helping style and bring the homes to life. Audrey thanks her family and husband, Todd Harris, for lending moral support while she pursues these projects, as well as for endless cups of tea to keep her moving forward throughout the sometimes laborious process of producing them. Chase couldn't accomplish anything without the encouragement of her friends, her far-flung pen pals who keep her company during long hours at the computer, and her family. Her four daughters, Addie, Jessie, Ross, and Katherine, amaze and inspire her every day; her husband, Charles, makes it all possible.

—CRE and AH

THE AUTHOR AND PHOTOGRAPHER

Photo by Jocelyn Knight Photography

Chase Reynolds Ewald has been writing about art, travel, design, food, and rustic style for more than twenty-five years. She is an active freelancer and the author of ten books. A graduate of Yale and the Graduate School of Journalism at U.C. Berkeley, she lives in northern California.

Photo by Susan Stella

Rooted in the dirt of the American West, Audrey Hall's photographs are formed by the unbridled spirit of its land. Her images about people and place are widely featured, from social campaigns to magazines and television. This is her twelfth book.

INTRODUCTION

The word *cabin* inevitably evokes a vision of a sturdy, modestly sized stacked-log structure, usually featuring a stone fireplace from which a curl of smoke wafts into the sky. This idyllic dwelling is typically envisioned as being tucked amongst trees, sometimes situated by a mountain stream and often with an enviable mountain or lake prospect—a true retreat.

One aspect of the enduring appeal of the cabin is that the more restrained the size and palette of the dwelling, the more one is open to and able to appreciate the nature within which it is immersed. Traditionally built with small windows and dark logs, it has long been characterized by dark and cavelike interiors, leaving it cut off from the outdoors. This was partly due to the limitations of the materials and partly by design: the more closed off from nature a cabin feels, the more it becomes a refuge from the elements.

The ideal of the cabin has transformed at a rapid pace in recent years due to evolutions in taste, patterns of use, and advances in technology. It no longer needs to be small, or cut off from the outdoors, or suffer from dark interiors. Today's cabins enjoy the best of both worlds. They are open to nature, with more glazing and doorways and outdoor living spaces, both covered and exposed to the elements. Yet they still retain a coziness and warmth that enhances the sense of their sheltering aspect.

Contemporary cabin style is expressed in a multitude of nontraditional, cabinlike structures. The elements of a cabin—wood, stone, sheltering eaves, cozy interiors, adjacent outdoor spaces—can be combined with nontraditional elements such as flat roofs, steel details, floor-to-ceiling glass, and aesthetic influences from around the world. The cabin ideal today might be expressed as a small house constructed of reclaimed wood and glass on a huge conservation property, furnished with a hint of eastern influence, and oriented toward its unique feature: in one case, natural hot springs and a phenomenal view of the Sawtooth Mountains. It can include a slopeside ski home imbued with color and unique verve, or, conversely, a European-influenced chalet striking in its sophistication and restraint. It might be a low-slung, 1950s repurposed ranch house featuring a long porch with rocking chairs, its window trim painted red to highlight the extraordinary Big Horn mountain views reflected in the glass. It could be a bespoke reclaimed timber home in which every item, from the building itself to stairs to metalwork, is handcrafted by master artisans. Alternatively, cabin style can be expressed in dramatic renovations of dated log homes from the 1990s; in such homes, a coat of black or white paint can utterly transform the spaces while highlighting the tactile nature of the log experience.

Kentucky-based designer Chuck Bolton furnished a stone and log cabin built by JLF Architects and Design Builders in a riparian meadow environment near the Jackson Hole elk refuge. A spring creek sprang

A reclaimed wood-and-stone cabin designed by JLF Architects and Design Builders on the edge of a natural meadow with rehabilitated riparian habitat suggests a timeless permanence. Interiors by Chuck Bolton of Lyle House Antiques are cozy and evocative, featuring many handcrafted details.

out of the ground just behind the house and flowed on to create safe harbors for trout: shallow pools and spawning beds which had been silted in but were restored under the new owners and their neighbors. This is not an environment into which one introduces new structures without great forethought and sensitivity. Says JLF Principal Paul Bertelli, "If you had to pick a sacred spot in Jackson, I'd have to venture that this would be on the list." In such a setting, says Chuck Bolton, "My first principle in interior design is to get out of the way."

In the same valley lives a larger home with a more modernistic expression. Designed by CLB Architects, its cabin style is expressed in reclaimed wood, posts and beams. Multihued corral boards help it blend into the landscape, while its rooflines echo the mountain peaks that frame it. Inside, high-end finishes, airy volumes, uncluttered interiors, and modern light fixtures suggesting a contemporary outlook are balanced with grounding beams and reclaimed materials.

Both homes capture the ethos of cabin style today. On the inside, the style is expressive, organic, changeable, and unique to the personalities who inhabit it. On the outside it is respectful of place and lives lightly in deference to the land.

"From the very beginning," says JLF's Bertelli, "we discuss what we see in the land so that the architecture doesn't lose an opportunity in the landscape, and the landscape doesn't lose an opportunity in the architecture."

In cabin style, interiors and exteriors work together to comprise one harmonious whole. Whether the expression is modern-leaning or a more literal reference to regional history, the result is the same: buildings that seem to belong.

Eric Logan, principal of CLB Architects, has spent his entire life in the West and is now raising his family there. As a result, he takes a long view; he has never lost sight of the context in which he designs. "We tend to speak about the work in plain language," he explains. "The grandeur of the landscape puts us in our place."

CLB Architects employed cabin elements in a transitional home with guesthouse. Working within neighborhood guidelines that favored more traditional styles, the exterior is a clean mountain-modern aesthetic of stonework, beams, reclaimed siding, and cedar shake roofs.

HOT SPRINGS HIDEAWAY

Northern Idaho is a wilderness paradise of wildlife, mountain ranges, trout-rich rivers and lakes, and high-elevation peaks. It includes the headwaters of multiple major rivers and is criss-crossed by National Scenic Byways. To say that its scenery is breathtaking would be an under-statement. Heart-stopping is more like it.

Into this mountain fastness, an empty nester with grown children and a love of tranquility alighted on a small property that might as well have been ten times larger for its sense of space, privacy, wildlife, and wilderness. To be there is to experience a complete immersion in nature; despite its proximity to the road, the avian life is so robust the birdsong drowns out all other noises. The property is inaccessible half the year except by snowmobile, so while most use occurs in the summertime, any construction would need to be sturdy and the compound self-sufficient enough so that someone snowed in during a blizzard could emerge unscathed a week later. The overriding factor for the owner was its strong sense of quiet, peace, and tran-quility. For that reason, she desired her own home separate from the other lodgings and outbuildings—just one in a compound designed to take advantage of the site's most unique feature, its natural hot springs.

The owner had extensive experience in homebuilding and design and had admired the work of Miller Roodell Architects for years. She told architect Candace Miller that she knew she wanted a rustic style, but a version of that style that would be an accurate reflection of who she was, of her interests and influences. An inveterate traveler and student of eastern philosophies, she was clear in expressing her desire to focus on the peace and relaxation found on the property. The overriding mood, she insisted, should be serenity. To that end, it was crucial that the house be simple, quiet in tone, and not overly ornamented or heavily furnished.

The property starts on the western edge of the broad, flat valley floor, on the fringes of a wetland. It rises up through sagebrush foothills whose contours allow for a sense of privacy and separation, not only from the main and access roads but from each other. Candace Miller and Miller Roodell project manager Chris Clay spent an inordinate amount of time working on the master plan in a conscientious effort to get the placement and sequencing just right. The goal was to create multiple buildings of modest size that would integrate within rather than dominate the landscape. They would be designed to take full advantage of the extraordinary views without drawing attention to themselves.

For a unique Idaho prop-erty blessed by natural hot springs, the owner tapped Miller Roodell Architects to design a multi-building compound in which her own home would be modest in scale and nestle into the landscape. "This is a place for the owner and her family to come to the area and be able to enjoy one another, play together and just be in the wild together," says architect Candace Miller. "Paying attention to scale was important in making the buildings fit the site." The 2,500-square-foot structure is built of stone and dovetailed logs and topped with a bonderized metal roof.

The entrance gate lies on the upper part of the property. The road drops down past a previously existing house, a barn with caretaker's quarters, a horse shed, a greenhouse, guest cabins, and the compound's South Camp, with its outdoor kitchen, changing-room pavilion, and boardwalk connectors leading to three pools fed by natural hot springs. It then continues down to the owner's home, which one approaches on foot through a small grove of aspens at the very base of the hillside where the wetlands meet the sagebrush hills.

The 2,500-square-foot structure is composed of stone and dovetailed logs and topped with a roof of bonderized metal. Purposefully scaled to the diminutive size of the owner, it has no wasted space. Designed on one level (except for the central gabled section, which creates an opportunity for a sleeping loft), it hugs the ground at the edge of the hillside. "The client wanted it to be warm, inviting, and able to accommodate a crowd. And she wanted the views to be primary," says Miller. "It was our idea to keep everything low slung to the landscape so it couldn't be spotted from the roadway. We wanted it to look like a homesteader cabin that might have already been there."

Despite its two guest rooms and loft, it was designed as the owner's hideaway, with the master suite separate from and on the far side of the main kitchen/living/dining space. Debra Shull and Phoebe McEldowney of Haven Interior Design worked closely with the owner on the home's interiors. "She wanted places in the house that had nothing, in order to celebrate the beauty of the architecture and its peacefulness," says Shull. "Her mandate to us was that everything in the house should have purpose and meaning." As a result, the furnishings include handmade Moroccan tiles and many antiques, some Balinese and some Asian. Throughout the home, antique Navajo, Turkish, and Moroccan rugs convey the feeling of age and add to the spiritual well-being of the house. A modern, clean-lined ethos defines the spaces despite the vintage feel conveyed by the low-ceilinged, reclaimed-wood entry,

At this family compound the emphasis is on the mountain views and hot springs. A natural-looking trio of pools was created off the owner's bedroom in a design conceived by an Onsen hot pool specialist in Japan and executed by DHM Landscape Design. Further up the hill, on the property's South Camp, another three pools are connected by boardwalks to an outdoor kitchen and changing-room pavilion.

reclaimed terra-cotta and oak floors, and items like the distressed hutch in the kitchen and claw-foot tub in one bathroom. Sheer draperies and natural fabrics such as linen, silk, and alpaca infuse the home with a luxurious, tactile quality.

The master bedroom suite, accessed via a quiet nook furnished with a desk, is a study in simplicity: a low bed on a built-in platform with a Balinese gate as a headboard and a window seat. A crystal chandelier adds a touch of sparkle and light; a restrained palette and the gold Buddha in the corner amplify the feeling of serenity. But with windows on three sides and a door to the private patio, it is all about the view across and up the valley, and of course the hot springs. Three gathering pools—a

cold plunge pool, a medium-temperature pool, and a hot pool— form a trio just off the roofed and trussed private patio. To soak in the healing minerals of the hot springs while admiring the mountain scenery or gazing at the stars, brilliant in the night sky, is to literally feel one with nature.

The project remains ongoing, and each addition is meant to harmonize with the land and existing architecture while respecting environmental tenets for pristine, irreplaceable areas. The challenge, says the architect, is to be as conscientious as possible about limiting the disturbance on the site. "You want to complement the land," says Clay, "rather than drop a marker on the site."

RIGHT: The low-ceilinged entry has a cozy, protected feel with its wood ceiling and beams. The Michael Coleman painting acts almost as a window in the enclosed space. The antique Balinese buffet is flanked by sconces from Always Antiques.

FACING: The living room with reclaimed beams centers on a stone fireplace with arched opening and wood mantel. A table designed by Haven Interiors rests on a vintage Heriz rug. The lamp is an antique from the 1920s.

The serene kitchen walks the line between rustic and refined. The Moroccan tile backsplash and quartzite countertop give a fresh, clean look, while the cabinet from Mulligans wears its patina well. Pendants were designed by Haven Interiors; hardware and faucet came from Rocky Mountain Hardware and Newport Brass, respectively. Skylights bathe the room in light, even on cloudy days.

RIGHT: A simple wooden ladder leads to a lofted space above the living room. A sleek steel box inset into the side of the fireplace provides wood storage.

FACING: The hallway to the master bedroom accommodates an office nook with a desk handcrafted by Hickory Furniture Designs. The chair is from Restoration Hardware. The small antique lamp adds a graceful note.

The homeowner wanted to emphasize tranquility throughout the home. The master bedroom is for repose, contemplation and enjoying the views. Furnishings are deliberately kept minimal with an antique chandelier and Moroccan rug and a vintage Balinese headboard and trunk. An alpaca throw adds warmth and a touch of luxury.

ABOVE: A bunk room charms with its curtained nook with built-in window seat tucked between built-in beds under a cozy low-beamed ceiling. Pendleton blankets and an antique Navajo rug speak to the home's place in the West.

FACING: In the modestly scaled guest bed and bath, a Rohl sink, Newport Brass faucet, Pottery Barn lamp, and Rose Tarlow table furnish with simplicity.

A Kohler claw-foot tub positioned by the window gives a retro feel to the almost spartan master bath.

The outdoor living room sees a lot of use in the summer, its antique daybed the perfect place for a rest. The chair, from Old Hickory, has a Donghia fabric cushion.

COLLECTED CABIN

Brad Beckworth is Texan through and through, but from the moment he read *Lonesome Dove* he knew he had to get to Montana. Fourteen years ago he went on a fly-fishing trip along the Yellowstone River with his father. As soon as he got back within cell reception, he called his wife to suggest they start looking at property. Stacey had never been to Montana, but when she visited she understood. "Once you see Montana, it's really love at first sight," she says. "It's the perfect place to teach your children about the important things in life, like family and nature."

The Beckworths spent fourteen years searching for the right piece of property and found it just outside Bozeman. Its 270 acres extend from the valley floor—with live water and wetlands, aspens and meadows—to forested foothills with expansive views. Despite its proximity to town, it has a decidedly agrarian feeling, with plentiful wildlife, a healthy fishery, and pasturelands and hayfields rather than visible neighbors. As a couple, the Beckworths had extensive experience in home building, and they'd learned much from Brad's mother, an interior designer. They chose Joe Roodell of Miller Roodell Architects to realize their vision: a cabin the family could live in while a barn and the main house underwent construction on the ridge. For the primary residence, they wanted a somewhat modern home with clean interiors and extensive glazing. They envisioned something very different for the guest cabin. It would be of the region, modestly scaled and historically appropriate. And rather than some reductive version of the main home, it would be original, textured, layered, and highly handcrafted.

In designing the cabin, the architect created a low, symmetrical, cross-axis structure tucked up near the wooded slope behind it and open to the view. A timbered gabled extension off the back forms a carport, while the front extension encompasses a covered patio overlooking a pond. Materially, the home is simple: wood siding, metal roof, stone chimney. "It's more refined than traditional rustic," observes Roodell. "Every stone was worked to get a tighter joint pattern and tighter layup overall." The matte finish and classic roofline, he adds, allow it to blend into the landscape.

A Texas couple spent fourteen years searching for the perfect site for a Montana home, finding it just outside Bozeman. A simple, serene palette unifies the rooms of the 1,200-square-foot home designed by Miller Roodell Architects. In the kitchen, furnishings curated by designer Abby Hetherington in partnership with the homeowner elevate this two-bedroom cabin from guesthouse to home. Details include Urban Electric pendants, Robert Ogden sconce, Rocky Mountain Cabinet Hardware, Ann Sacks tile backsplash, and a custom hood by the builder, Bolton Construction.

The 1,200-square-foot interior is simple and serene, with metal countertops, a Montana moss rock fireplace, a concrete floor, and reclaimed wood on the walls, ceilings, and cabinets. Designer Abby Hetherington of Hetherington Interiors credits the builder, fifth-generation carpenter Cass Bolton of Bolton Custom Homes, for hand-picking uniformly gray wood panels for the interior and multicolored panels for the exterior. Outside, the color is warmer, while the uniform tone of the interior creates both a quiet cohesiveness and an appropriate backdrop for decor with verve.

The furnishings represent a curated collection. Despite the cabin's demure size, there are unexpected moments in fabrics, art, furniture, lighting, and tile. One bathroom has Aztec-leaning floor tiles; the other has a custom-made textured concrete trough sink with a movable barn-board divider. Throughout the cabin, collectible items like vintage photographs and Montana history books abound, the product of thoughtful collecting on the part of both interior designer and client. Hetherington considers collecting a significant part of her job; she begins as soon as she understands the clients' lives and an often fictional backstory for the structure. Meanwhile, Stacey Beckworth is a passionate and knowledgeable collector with considerable experience and a seasoned eye. She tracked down books and Yellowstone Park memorabilia from area antique stores and auctions. She made repeated trips to the Round Top Antiques Fair in Texas to buy lights and rugs. She and Hetherington spent days working on lighting concepts, as well as brainstorming creative ways to repurpose found objects.

A guest cabin can be an encapsulation of the main home's material palette and tenets, or it can be a retreat that celebrates the romance of place. The challenge remains how to infuse one with character, personality, and soul. Hetherington suggested treating the guest cabin as an entity of its own rather than a smaller-scale iteration of the main house or a repository for leftover art and furniture. She incorporated localized artifacts to give a sense of history and legacy, although for upholstered furnishings, it was all about durability. And it should be fun, the designer adds, with a nod to playfulness: there might be candy dishes set out, or games left half played.

This collaboration between architect, designer, builder, and client resulted in a structure that is small in scale but expansive enough for entertaining. It is appropriate to the area without calling attention to itself. And despite some modern touches, it feels rooted in history and decidedly of its place, with its barn-board exterior hearkening back to the agricultural roots of the neighborhood. "We wanted the cabin to feel collected and we wanted people to feel kind of nostalgic when they were there," says the owner. "We wanted them to feel at home."

Architect Joe Roodell collaborated closely with the owners on the design, a low, symmetrical cross-axis structure that is nestled at the base of the treed foothills and enjoys a view over the open valley. The two-bedroom, two-bath home works well for the owners, while a barn and main home are constructed higher up the ridge off the valley floor.

ABOVE: A blue Kelly Wearstler chair pops against the rugged but refined stacked-stone fireplace. To achieve clean lines, "Every stone was worked to get a tighter layup," says architect Joe Roodell. The open shelving is of reclaimed wood.

RIGHT: The living room opens up to a covered patio, which looks across a pond to the peaks beyond. A shearling chair and oversized lighting pendant decline to compete with the view. The owner scouted Montana antiques shops and the Round Top Antiques Fair in Texas for collectibles that impart a sense of history.

LEFT: Each bedroom has a cozy window seat, built-in cabinets, Warhol art, a rope chandelier, and a luxurious bed with a view.

ABOVE: An orange Saba Italia chair pops against subdued tones in a bathroom, while antler pendants from Fish's Antler Art provide an organic touch. The custom-designed concrete trough sink has a movable wood shelf.

ABOVE: Rich tones and varied textures make the bedroom a refuge. Collectible art includes Andy Warhol's buffalo nickel.

FACING ABOVE AND BELOW: The second bathroom has reclaimed-wood pocket doors, blue cabinets set against graphic tile from Sabine Hill, and an arrowhead lighting fixture.

BIG HORN
CAMP STYLE

The town of Big Horn, Wyoming, represents the best of both worlds. It lies close to Sheridan's big-town amenities but offers a rural lifestyle and a decidedly small-town feel. The community is defined by its location off the main road, tucked up against the east slope of the Big Horn Mountains and abutting the million-plus-acre Big Horn National Forest. There, the proximity to wilderness and its protected quality of life is unparalleled.

For one couple, ranchers and horse breeders who spend most of the year in Texas, it was Sheridan's world-famous polo club that originally drew them to the area. But it was in Big Horn that they found what was, for them, the perfect property: more land than house, with plenty of room for horses. Best of all, it came with a vintage building that could be restored with its authentic western charm intact.

According to Larry Baker of A&K Construction in Sheridan, previous visitors had declared the building a teardown. But for the buyers, the low-slung bunkhouse-like structure was a big part of the property's appeal. Admittedly, it had been haphazardly constructed in the 1950s or '60s. The foundation was minimal, the porch was flimsy, the second story barely usable with ceilings too low to stand upright. But the couple liked its scale, its appropriateness, and the way it was sited on the property in deference to its agricultural neighbors and the greater landscape. Its prospect—looking west toward the Big Horn Mountains and south over open pastures to grassy foothills vibrant with wildlife—was breathtaking.

Upon acquiring the property, the couple retained architect Dan Stocker to develop a concept that would save the soul of the house but make it usable and comfortable for everyday living. Architect Dennis Deppmeier of 2North, who has a background in historic preservation, was brought on to carry Stocker's ideas forward and develop the interior architecture. Jeremiah Young of design firm Kibler & Kirch joined the team to infuse the structure with unique elements and timeless handcrafted appeal.

First the roof was replaced and the upper level rebuilt with a staggered roofline; this broke up the monolithic lines while giving two-thirds of the house space for a second story. Dormers were then added to allow for human-scaled bedrooms and baths. The architects introduced reclaimed wood and river rock treatment on the exterior and reclaimed fir on the dormers to help the structure blend into the landscape. Standing

In the tiny town of Big Horn, Wyoming, a vintage rustic ranch house received a thorough renovation with a focus on handcrafted authenticity.

The largest volume of the home—an open-concept living, dining, and kitchen space—manages to be both inviting and cozy with rugs, stone, and wood elements combining in perfect harmony. Though the structure is modestly scaled, its dining table can accommodate twelve.

RIGHT: On the long, low-slung porch the Big Horn Mountain view reflects dramatically in the glass while red-trimmed windows enliven the home's facade.

BELOW: Six organically shaped Old Hickory Grove Park Rockers line the welcoming and functional covered porch. The rockers—a classic design produced since 1913—provide the perfect complement to the stone and wood. The porch adapts well to seasons and a variety of functions: eating, working, and relaxing after a day on the range or the polo field.

dead logs were added to support the porch, which was first removed and then reconstructed for functionality and longevity. The new porch retains the bunkhouse style, running much of the length of the building, and helps preserve its vintage look, complete with red trim windows. In clement weather, the porch is the staging place for the day's activities and, at the end of an active day, the preferred venue for unwinding.

Appropriately, the focal point of the home is the river rock fireplace that anchors one end of the great room. The area includes a dining space and is open to the kitchen for ease of entertaining. The ground floor also encompasses the master bedroom suite, a roomy corner office with big views, and a utilitarian combination mudroom and laundry room defined by handmade clay Saltillo tiles from Mexico. Upstairs, two bedrooms share a bath and open sitting room with views over meadows to the mountains. Throughout, the spaces are cozy and snug without feeling cramped and are characterized by a feeling of solidity, honesty, and authenticity.

This sense of authenticity derives from the extraordinary level of detail found from exterior to interior, from treatments to furnishings. Reclaimed fir doors and floors were wire brushed for a tactile quality and distressed feel. All cabinets were custom built of reclaimed wood by Mark Sevier of Dovetail Designs & Millwork; for the twig mosaic design on the refrigerator door, architect Dennis Deppmeier collected the willow by hand along the edges of Pryor Creek in Montana. Steve Blood of Penrose Design in New York handcrafted the lighting to the designers' specifications, while Montana blacksmith Frank Annighofer hand-forged the strap hinges and other iron elements found throughout the house.

Before settling in Big Horn, the couple had spent time on a classic dude ranch outside Cody, Wyoming, where they'd been introduced to furniture by the exuberant, often whimsical western stylist Thomas Molesworth, whose works define the traditional school of western style today. When presenting to the team a portfolio of interiors that spoke to them, Deppmeier recalls, the clients' preferred style was strongly reminiscent of the '30s and '40s dude-ranch era that represented the designer's heyday. As a result, from lighting to furniture, many items commissioned for the home were directly inspired by Molesworth. Taken together, they incorporate all the elements of his timeless design language: iron, leather, applied pole, Navajo rugs, Pendleton blankets, brass nailheads, fringe, burl, and beadwork.

The handmade furniture includes numerous pieces from Old Hickory Furniture, which has been using the same handcrafting techniques since 1899, as well as Molesworth reproductions by Marc Taggart of Cody, Wyoming, such as the hand-beaded magazine rack. The owners' art collection—including Ansel Adams photographs in leather frames, paintings by Howard Post and Glenn Dean, and a collection of Edward Borein etchings—informed many of the spaces, guiding the overall palette as well as selections in new and antique rugs.

The beauty in this understated ranchlike abode reveals itself slowly in its solidity, its details, and its unique handcraftedness. The home, says Jeremiah Young, "is modest from a certain perspective. But everything is made by hand—every screw, every light fixture, all the hardware. The house is small, but no expense was spared, no corners were cut. The approach was entirely authentic and handmade. They probably should have started from scratch," he adds, "but they didn't because they wanted it to be as authentic as possible."

The home was designed with restraint in terms of size, yet it still has transitional areas and a number of intimate spaces for reflection and solitude. Future plans for the property include converting an old grain barn to a guest cabin and developing a pond and an equestrian facility. But for now, the family has found, when you have a porch with a view, and a cozy interior to retreat to, not much more is really needed.

FACING: Timelessly stylish custom Molesworth chairs from Marc Taggart in Cody, Wyoming, are grouped in conversation with a leather Chesterfield sofa. The hand-painted ceiling light, beaded magazine rack, burled lamp, and Old Hickory side table represent equal parts art and function.

ABOVE: Polo trophies, etchings, and leather details enhance this masculine study. After the rebuild, bigger openings allow for more light and a sweeping view of the Big Horns. The long Molesworth desk is by Marc Taggart, western sofa from McKinley Leather, and tooled ottoman and lamps by Old Hickory. The oversized "Walk in Beauty" rug anchors and grounds the space.

LEFT: A Glenn Dean oil painting above a carved-front Hickory Chair chest provides a focal point at one end of the dining space.

The rustic kitchen designed by Jeremiah Young of Kibler & Kirch achieves perfect balance in scale. All hardware, metal work, and lighting are handmade custom works. The twig mosaic refrigerator door adds patterned depth to the natural textures. The space is intimate, yet there is ample room to cook and gather. The lively, colorful rug is by Southwest Looms.

ABOVE: Each upstairs bedroom includes additional sleeping space via built-in wooden beds with views of the Big Horns. Pendleton blankets, pillows, and layered rugs add to the charm. An antique metal coat stand, leather Gunnison Chair by Hickory Chair, and tooled leather ottoman prove useful and comfortable.

FACING: In the master bedroom reading area, designers from Kibler & Kirch transformed an uninspiring cabinet by introducing nailheads and hand painting in keeping with the colorful oil painting by Howard Post. Woven leather ottoman and bed from Tables & More, distressed leather chairs by Classic Leather.

ABOVE: A combined mudroom and laundry has handmade Mexican Saltillo tiles on the floor and counter, a carefully camouflaged washer and dryer, and a long bench to perch on when removing boots.

FACING: The master bathroom reveals consistent artistry and level of craft in cabinets, hardware, tile, and lighting. There is nothing oversized or out of human scale; the space celebrates function and the inherent beauty of items made by human hands.

FACING: A custom-built La Lune bar cabinet picks up on panel details in the adjacent kitchen. Only a step away from the comfortable seating of the living room, it creates an intimate and inviting place to relax.

LEFT: Organic details in the railing and screen, collected mounts, handmade sconces, and an antique Afghan runner enhance the simple stairwell in a home where every space offers an opportunity to enjoy thoughtful design and well-crafted details.

Achieving the sought-after balance, says architect Justin Tollefson, lies in superior craftsmanship and detailing. This creates an environment that is rich and luxurious but still serene, he explains. "We were trying to do that and I think we were successful. It carries through to railings, trim, even the doors: two squares of reclaimed set within the frame, which creates a shadow and a craftsmanlike effect but is still very simple. Our approach was almost to pretend the house was already there and that we were remodeling it, starting with the concept of 'simple, efficient, and with a stacked floor plan.'

"In the end," he adds, "the house is interesting and luxurious but in a very simple context. You don't have to make things complicated to make them beautiful."

RIGHT: On Site Management contractors employed all their skills as craftsmen in the building of the chalet, particularly evident in the woodwork details.

FACING: As is typical of chalet design, the main entrance is on the lowest level. In this sheltered area, the handcrafted appeal of wood and stone is palpable. An organic bench softens the otherwise austere space.

ABOVE: The staircase rises through three levels in the center of the house, making a graceful artistic statement in its original scrollwork. The antler chair with sheepskin is one of a kind.

RIGHT: The great room is anchored at one end by the kitchen, at the other by the clean-edged fireplace with limestone surround. The handblown glass deer sculpture above the mantel is by Simone Crestani. The sofa-back timber console is a custom-made piece sourced out of Utah. On the built-in bench, C&C Milano fabric.

and modular sofa by Baxter, grounds the room without interfering with the view. Alpaca window treatments add softness and texture to the large volume. Kelly Wearstler swivel chairs can be spun around to enjoy the scenery.

FACING: A modern approach is evident in the kitchen's open shelving, concrete countertops, and earth-toned handmade dinnerware. The reclaimed white oak cabinets were hand-built by On Site Management.

LEFT: A maple-slab oval dining table with Kelly Wearstler chairs in a muted but festive striped Dedar upholstery comfortably seats ten. The BDDW credenza is wrapped in leather.

BELOW: Zellige terra-cotta tiles, Watermark fixtures, Ochre counter stools and a painting by Theodore Waddell imbue the kitchen and dining nook with a refined elegance.

FACING: A family lounge area adjoining the master bedroom suite and children's rooms offers a private space removed from the bustle of the public rooms. A cowhide-topped coffee table from Verellen and a spare rope chandelier nod to local history. The serene painting is by Chris Maynard.

ABOVE: A Cloud chandelier from Apparatus floats above the quiet master bedroom, whose bed is draped with Mark Alexander linen. The painting is by Matt Flint; rug is a luxurious sheepskin.

FACING: Arteriors sconces, a Waterworks wall-mounted, unlacquered brass faucet, and a slim-profile mirror complete a rustic sleek bathroom. Baskets provide texture and a sculptural presence on open shelves.

ABOVE LEFT: The shower and steam room, inspired by Turkish baths, has concrete tile inlay sourced from Cle tile and hammam bowls custom made in Turkey. The L'aviva Home pendant casts graphic shadows.

ABOVE RIGHT: A sculptural Victoria and Albert soaking tub with a Waterworks filler and soft draperies create a spa-like refuge for a bath.

RIGHT: The bunk room celebrates efficient use of space with built-in beds and bookcases filled with vintage thermoses and children's books. Coral and Tusk pillows, Pendleton striped blankets, a whimsical wood light fixture, and fabric elk mounts speak to the West.

FACING: A twin room offers a fresh take on the western ski house aesthetic—and a cool loft accessed by a ladder.

ON THE EDGE OF RUSTIC

I t is one thing to create a compound on a ranch; it's quite another to create the sense of a compound on a mostly level site on the edge of a golf course. But his clients were specifically *not* interested in a starter castle, says architect John Lauman of JLF Architects and Design Builders. Rather, they were seeking a more modestly scaled presence in what would be their full-time home. They would use the layout of buildings to create a sense of arrival, screen out neighbors, and direct one's gaze to the primary southern views over open space to the Snake River Range. And they would use multiple structures, mostly attached, to create privacy and a sense of separation within the larger whole.

The homeowners, recently retired and still very active outdoorspeople, were relocating to Jackson, Wyoming, from the East Coast when they chose their site and retained JLF Architects to design their home. Enthusiastically involved from the beginning, they even rented a house nearby to live in while the construction was taking place.

Originally conceived as a somewhat U-shaped structure (parking courtyard within the U, and big views over open landscape to the south, on the opposite side of the building) with a guest cabin connected by a covered walkway, the design expanded and evolved over the course of the project. What was intended as the guesthouse became the husband's office and retreat, while the self-contained guest quarters moved across the driveway to the corner of the property. Meanwhile, the covered walkway to the guesthouse-now-man-cave became a glass connector—separate but attached, with shelter from the elements and a major "Aha!" moment experienced en route as one glimpses the mountain view.

The arrival sequence brings one to the front door, which is located underneath a gabled porch in the center of the main mass of the reclaimed timber and cedar-shake-roofed house. A low stone wall creates a division between the structure and driveway, with the barnlike garage wing to the right. To the left, the attached log-cabin office retreat enjoys its own entryway. The low, glass-walled, metal-roofed connector links it to the main volume while lightening the mass by offering transparency and views of the mountains straight from the driveway.

Upon entering the house, the simple stone-floored foyer reveals true stacked log corners in a nod to the origin of the reclaimed materials. The "announcement of place" happens as one's gaze travels straight

A Jackson, Wyoming home designed by JLF Architects and Design Builders and built by their construction partner, Big-D Construction, uses reclaimed materials and dramatic scissor trusses to establish sense of place in a compound-like home with views of the Snake Mountains.

through the living room to the long prospect south, creating a pause before entering the great room. This is important because, once in the great room, dramatic scissor trusses of heavily distressed reclaimed material dominate the space and draw the eye upward.

"We find that a truss is nice in dividing a volume," explains the architect. "Historically a truss is a horizontal bottom cord; this was mostly out of necessity and ease of construction. But a bottom cord is sometimes too close to the human scale." In this case, the choice of truss generates energy while creating a greater sense of volume than would have been possible with a horizontal timber. The unexpected truss structure creates a powerful architectural moment within the vaulted-ceilinged space and acts as a counterpoint to the weight of the expansive view.

From the main living, dining, and kitchen area, the bedrooms radiate out, even into a second level over the garage, while the master bedroom suite juts out to the south toward the intermittently treed open space. This is mirrored by the husband's retreat, constructed almost as if a separate cabin, a move reflected in its heavy, lodgelike ambience. The simple gabled form is oriented away from the house toward the view and enjoys its own shed-roofed porch, which overlooks a hot tub and shallow pond with partial deck. Verdone Landscape Architects were tasked with creating the water feature whose cascades provide the soothing sound of water while the pond, depending on the season, creates the effect of a winter wonderland or summertime idyll.

For the interiors, designer Jet Zarkadas of Los Griegos Studio in Santa Fe helped the owners balance the masculine and the feminine, the heavily rustic with the more refined, and the family's East Coast past with its new west present. She assisted the husband in creating his den retreat, with its elaborate bar, cigar smoking accoutrements, and animal mounts. With the wife she scoured their existing collection of furniture, selecting pieces that could make the transition to mountain living. A statement rug crafted from hides in a stylized pattern referencing Navajo design grounds the living room and became the base upon which the rest of the space takes its cues. Zarkadas says the water-referencing tones found throughout the house speak to the owners' longtime passion for the Turks and Caicos islands, as well as their previous coastal home. The kitchen is a study in serenity with Shaker-inspired, frame-and-panel reclaimed fir cabinets, greenish-gray Pietra Cardosa countertops, oak floors, and a glazed Fireclay tile backsplash in a tranquil pale aqua. In bedrooms and the guesthouse, there is a sophisticated simplicity and comfort in the human-scaled spaces. The goal, says the designer, was "a refined mountain elegance."

The home succeeds in balancing its different personas—mountain and coast, rustic and refined—by establishing a strong sense of place through its materiality and authenticity. "We strive for truth in materials," explains Lauman. "If there's log, it needs corners. If there's stone veneer, the wall needs to be thick enough that it could be a stone wall." In a log cabin-like wing, windows must be historically appropriate, double hung rather than casement. To that end, new white oak floors were treated for an aged look, while walls, beams, and kitchen cabinets were made of reclaimed wood. Having master craftsmen such as those from Big-D Construction, JLF Architects' construction partner, executing the details makes all the difference, as does the sense of place conveyed by the work of Wyoming blacksmith Jeff Morris, who created much of the hardware, light fixtures, chandeliers, and fireplace doors. The solidity and tactile nature of hand-forged metal and antique materials imbues the home with a palpable regional authenticity—establishing this cabinlike compound firmly within its setting on the edge of rustic.

FACING ABOVE: In the entry, the true stacked-log corners make an artist statement with a chandelier by Jeff Morris. The entry table and low bench were designed by LGS and made by Hands of America in Santa Fe.

FACING BELOW: The elegant kitchen marries Shaker-inspired frame-and-panel reclaimed fir cabinets with greenish-gray Pietra Cardosa countertops and a glazed Fireclay tile backsplash. Ocean tones found throughout the house reference the couple's love of the sea.

ABOVE: Stylistically, the husband leaned rustic, the wife more refined. A compromise was for him to have his own retreat—separate but attached—which is more weighty, masculine, and traditional than the rest of the house.

FACING: Tranquility reigns in a guest bedroom with a crisp blue-and-white color scheme, brass beds set against white walls, and simple wood-trimmed windows. In a bathroom with a fresh outlook, mountain views draw the eye.

The house takes advantage of its situation at the edge of a development by facing the views and orienting on the shallow, swimmable pond. It can be reached directly from the husband's lair, with its private porch, as well as from the main home's patio.

RIGHT: The narrow, glass-walled connector acts like a bridge and makes the most of the views while giving the den the feel of a separate cabin.

BELOW: The handcrafted appeal of the home is evident in the approach to the husband's retreat, which enjoys a private entry from the parking area.

The comfortable guesthouse was placed a stone's throw away on the far edge of the driveway for its own views and for privacy, creating a small ranchlike compound.

BLUEBIRD POWDER DAY

Mountain homes tend to be characterized by their materials, usually log, timber, and stone. In a ski house for a young family within Montana's Yellowstone Club, it is glass—applied judiciously, strategically, and creatively—and a touchstone shade of blue that sets the tone for a contemporary approach to the ski-cabin experience.

This approach is announced at the home's entrance. Set within a traditional mountain architectural facade, a blue door is flanked by tall, narrow windows with trim in the same color. The entrance opens into a jewel-box foyer: dusky blue walls matching the front door; a luxurious sheepskin pouf ottoman and matching chair on modern legs; a white lacquer console with gold-toned hardware; a metallic chandelier; and one serene black-and-white painting of aspen trunks in snow. This low-ceilinged, curated experience allows for the joy of discovery in a transitional space before one is drawn into the great room. As the guest moves into the heart of the home, propelled by its sense of space, its remarkable vaulted ceiling and a picture-perfect view of Lone Mountain centered in the window, there's a double-take moment. Three panels of glass set into the wood floor force one's attention away from the view. One looks down and there is the briefest of moments before realizing the floor is glass (rather than, say, a gaping hole). This provokes a frisson of adrenaline, an instinctive reaction to the fear of falling. The scenario, then, is this: One is propelled forward by the promise of the spectacular room and view ahead, stopped abruptly, caught by the surprise, made to laugh. When one does eventually enter the great vaulted space, it is made even grander for having had one's attention interrupted. The glass floor is fun, it's unexpected, and it sets up the newcomer for the experience of the house.

The trick panels, however, are merely a precursor to the big move. The defining feature within the house is a three-story glass staircase. Beautiful, sculptural, and precision crafted, on a practical level it serves as a light well and ties the three stories together. On an aesthetic level it creates drama and promise. And it sends a clear message: This is not just another mountain house.

The high-elevation structure (at 8,500 feet) was designed by Corey Kelly of Locati Architects in a traditional refined rustic style appropriate to the neighborhood, with reclaimed-wood siding, reclaimed timbers

Within an outwardly traditional home designed by Locati Architects at Montana's Yellowstone Club, surprises abound. Architect Corey Kelly and Susie Hoffman of Envi Design collaborated closely with the owners to craft a custom experience, one with vibrancy and verve. It starts at the entry, with Mongolian sheep wool Baxter chairs, a Terzani chandelier, and a console designed by Envi and fabricated by Earth Elements set against a blue paint from Sherwin Williams called Moscow Midnight. The Glacier rug is from Rosemary Hallgarten, the artwork a photograph by Tracie Spence.

and trusses, and stone. It is built for comfort and, in classic ski-house style, is able to accommodate a crowd: It has seven bedrooms (including two bunkrooms) over three levels, each with its own relationship to the outdoors.

For the interiors, the owners brought in Susie Hoffman of Envi Interior Design Studio to execute a complete bespoke customization, from the macro—the glass staircase—to the micro, such as hardware. Hoffman worked closely with her clients throughout the project. "This family has a strong passion for Montana and it was so enjoyable to work with them," she says. "They have a vibrant sensibility and approached the project in a way that was fun and whimsical."

The fun appears in elements like the blue kitchen island, doorbells made of chairlift cable, charismatic and playful lighting fixtures, and contemporary art pieces. Striking and unusual colors, patterns, and textures can be found in tile in the living room wet bar, in the bathrooms, and in the kitchen—where, in an unexpected application, the tiles extend from the backsplash, travel around a corner, and continue up to the edge of the ceiling. A neon sign urges, "Choose Happy!"

The whimsy makes its play in bold graphic wallpapers in the bunk rooms and guest rooms, fabric "mounts," and a meticulously executed ski wall. In a brilliant play on retro ski cabins, where old skis are often mounted on walls as decor, Hoffman enlisted her husband, blacksmith and furniture maker Ira Cuelho, to craft an art piece at the base of the glass stairs. Two rows, one facing up, one facing down, of edge-to-edge skis are carefully arranged in an undulating chevron pattern. Hoffman spent hours searching for vintage skis (they had to have been manufactured before curved silhouettes were introduced) in the right length and, together with her husband, balancing the resulting colors and patterns when aligned. The statement is fresh, bold, and contemporary while speaking to the ski-house experience in a new and unexpected way.

Creativity is important, but comfort was a key driver of design throughout the house. Furnishings needed to be both luxurious and durable (this is, after all, a ski house, meant to handle a lot of people and activity and able to tolerate ski wear, clunky cowboy boots, excited kids, and food in the living room). This was balanced by touches of glamour which make an appearance in the foyer chandelier and lacquered console, the tufted suede seating in the mudroom, the vivid magenta fabric on dining chairs and living room ottomans (designed to conveniently tuck under the coffee table), and the Lucite bed in the master bedroom.

Architect Corey Kelly credits the homeowners for bringing energy and style to the project; he recalls "a huge Pinterest board and a million different ideas." For an interior designer, says Susie Hoffman, it was a dream collaboration. "This was a project where I could really stretch my legs," she says. "They were open to so many cool ideas, and came up with so many cool ideas of their own."

It's the result of this attitude that led to the installation of a kid-friendly trapdoor creating a secret passageway from a bunkroom to the great room above. When considered in conjunction with the custom leather poker table, it seems this house offers something for everyone—whether they're staying in by the fire or bursting out from the ski room in pursuit of what became the guiding motif for the house: the ultimate bluebird powder day.

The kitchen is scaled for family gatherings and entertaining, while a photograph by Nine Francois draws the eye down the hallway. Blue tones extend throughout the space—on the base of the kitchen island, in the tiles, and on the leather banquette cushions. The placement of the outdoor lounge adjacent to the kitchen and dining room gives it the feel of another room and makes it a natural extension of the indoor areas.

FACING: The vaulted great room is centered on a drop-dead view of Lone Mountain. There, two comfortable A. Rudin chairs face the view. The unexpectedly bright Bernhardt Design poufs tuck under an Envi-designed coffee table fabricated by Earth Elements. The sofas are from Baxter; the rug is Tai Ping.

ABOVE: The built-in bar in the corner of the living room combines Walker Zanger tile and sconces from Apparatus. The graceful backs of the Bon Bon stools from Berman Rosetti add a sculptural touch.

LEFT: The dining area enjoys immediate outdoor access and 180-degree views of the mountainscape. Magenta houndstooth fabric on chairs from Bright Furniture pop against the gray of the Madeline Weinrib hand-knotted silk rug. The Tod Von Mertens maple buffet, stained silver, separates the dining and living areas. The bear-on-cabin painting by Anke Schofield is a custom commission.

ABOVE: Diners benefit from a dinner setting curated by Envi atop a maple slab table under the Calla Mobile chandelier from John Pomp.

ABOVE: Tubs from Blu Bathworks are centered on the view. One bathroom has custom concrete countertops with integral sinks by Elements Concrete. The spa-like master bath combines a graphic-patterned tile with a black travertine floor, Taj Mahal countertops, and a Terzani chandelier.

ABOVE: In the junior master bedroom a Poltrona Frau bed is topped with custom-designed bedding by Envi. The rug is by Angela Adams, the Redondo chair is by Moroso. The painting by Robert McCauly is centered over a gas fireplace that has been elevated to the level of the bed.

LEFT: Playful, whimsical style is on vivid display in the lively bunkroom, where beds custom designed by Envi are accessed by an ombre stair. Envi also designed the bedding; the fabrics and wallpaper are from Spoonflower. Bernhardt Design made the Mitt Chair.

FACING: The guest room has fun with shape and texture through wallpaper from Knoll and a rug from Madeline Weinrib. Envi designed the bedding, as well as the deer mounts, which were made by Near and Dear.

ABOVE: A unique glass staircase runs through all three floors, serving as an artistic statement and carrying light throughout the home's interiors.

BELOW: An art wall of '80s-vintage skis was custom made by the designer's husband, artisan Ira Cuelho. The custom card table in the rec room was designed by Envi and fabricated by local craftsmen Russ Fry and Brian Pickering.

ABOVE: The outdoor living area has the feel of a comfortable lounge, with furnishings from Sutherland, dining for eight, a massive fire pit, and a killer view.

BIG HOLE RIVER REFUGE

Twenty-five years ago, a husband and wife from L.A. were traveling through the tiny town of Twin Bridges, Montana, when they pulled up in front of a fly-fishing shop. There the enthusiast behind the counter told them of an iconic fishing lodge in the area. They booked a stay—and returned every year for fifteen years. "We fell in love with Montana," the husband recalls. "The sky, the light, the colors, the people, the pace of life."

It was perhaps inevitable that they would start looking for property of their own in the same region, where the Ruby, Beaverhead, and Big Hole rivers come together to form the Jefferson River. This creates a rich breeding ground for trophy-size trout, yet the area is devoid of elbow-to-elbow swarms of fishermen on the riverbanks. In southwest Montana, there's room to spread out.

Fifteen years later, they were driving with a realtor in the lower Big Hole Valley, the husband recalls, when he told the driver to stop the car. "I got out and looked and said, 'This is it.'" When the realtor suggested they first view the ranch and existing buildings (none quite ready to be lived in), he said there was no need; he already knew. "It was the property itself, the way it was situated, the cottonwoods, the greenness, the alfalfa, and the mile of Big Hole River frontage. Everything about it was perfect. It spoke to me."

The existing home and barnlike storage building were usable with a little fixing up and adding on, and the family set about making the land their own. Conservation-minded outdoorspeople, they stocked the two ponds with rainbow and German brown trout and released ring-necked pheasants into the meadows. The land and riparian habitat were in good shape, having not been degraded by grazing livestock. A local husband and wife, the wife having lived for part of her childhood on that very ranch, were available as caretakers, ensuring a unique level of attention and trust. Over the ensuing years, however, as the owners' four grown children started having children of their own, the addition to the main house (in spite of its eight-bed bunkroom) was suddenly over capacity. It was time to expand.

The owner asked L.A. architect Bill Read, a college friend with whom he'd worked before, to create the initial concept for a guesthouse. Henri Foch of Instrinsik Architecture was retained to translate the vision to reality. The result of the collaboration was the 900-square-foot Buffalo Cabin. Made almost entirely

In a pair of cabins on Montana's Big Hole River, the experience is all about texture, in reclaimed wood walls, vintage textiles, interesting art, and antiques. One bedroom is furnished with vintage Navajo rugs, old handcrafted hay rakes, and a Victorian-era brass-and-iron headboard, which interior designer Laura Fedro had recrafted to accommodate a king-size bed. The antique side table was found in Butte; the vintage brass lamp has a Foss rawhide lampshade. Mounted above the bed is a collection of Haynes photographs from Yellowstone National Park.

of local Montana stone, it has a central stone fireplace, a generous porch on two sides, and a shed roof supported by hand-hewn timbers. As befits a cabin, its form is simple: a symmetrical rectangular double-height box with a central ridge beam—though large, modern-profile, red-painted windows with reclaimed wood headers comprise a nod to modernity. Completed in 2010, it is an efficient space. The bedroom is open to a compact kitchen with a small round table, while a loft with twin beds overlooks the living area below.

Set perpendicular to the first cabin and a short distance away (with a shared fire pit and horseshoe court between them), the 1,500-square-foot Moose Cabin, so named for the denizens of the wild who regularly wander past, was completed in 2017. This structure speaks to its partner cabin yet exhibits its own distinct character. Constructed of stone and reclaimed barnwood, its form is similar to the first but has a small porch on one side, a single dormer on the opposite side, and a single-story extension under a shed roof. This cabin, built to house a family comfortably, has a full living area open to a kitchen with a dining table that can seat eight, plus two bedrooms, two bathrooms, and an upstairs sleeping loft.

The interiors of both cabins are designed for texture, warmth, and authenticity, conveyed through reclaimed timber walls and floors. They incorporate traditional plaster surfaces and custom cabinets for a quiet, restful space. Interior designer Laura Fedro concentrated on curating vintage furnishings and art objects, many from the immediate region, while collaborating with the owners to source appropriate pieces. The cabins are furnished with antique painted furniture, iron bedsteads and farm implements, and period textiles such as Navajo rugs and Pendleton blankets. The owners' art—they are avid longtime collectors—ranges from early twentieth-century paintings by Birger Sandzen and vintage prints from the Haynes Photo Shops in Yellowstone to nineteenth-century Utah pottery. Contemporary pieces include striking oils by artist Logan Maxwell Hagege, who combines traditional subject matter with bold use of color.

Sited on a gentle rise in the river's bottomland near a tranquil rush-ringed pond, the cabins share quiet views across meadows and foothills to the sunrise and, from upstairs windows, euphoric views of the Pioneer Mountains across the tops of cottonwoods to the west. Unlike much new construction,

The cabins, designed by L.A. architect Bill Read and Henri Foch of Intrinsik Architecture, feature local stone and reclaimed wood. Situated on a gentle rise on the edge of hay meadows near a rush-ringed pond, they share a fire pit, a horseshoe court—and extraordinary views.

ABOVE: A roomy wraparound porch furnished with antique wicker, hayracks, and trunk promotes convivial moments.

RIGHT: A painting by Logan Maxwell Hegege pops amidst the subdued tones of leather furniture and antique items, like the collection of vintage jugs on the coffee table.

they seem rooted in their site. Architect Henri Foch credits the success of the project to the combination of craftsmanship and setting, its drama due to the contrast between the aridity of the surrounding high desert and the lush wildlife-rich ecosystem of the river bottom, all surrounded by snow-capped mountains. Equally crucial are the materials, specifically local Montana stone, which ties the buildings to the land, and reclaimed wood from historic structures. These, he says, impart authenticity and historic integrity.

The meticulous handcrafted detail found in both structures is the work of project manager Gordon Edsall and his team from JDL Construction. Their thoughtful, craftsmanlike approach resulted in buildings that belong. Fedro says they are like living, breathing structures; as such, they will not only endure for generations but age beautifully as they do.

The property sees a lot of use from June into the fall and carries cattle through the winter months. Every Labor Day, the extended family—which includes four kids and thirteen grandchildren—comes together to fish, to play, to relax in each other's company, to connect, and to get grounded again.

"It's become a gathering place and a refuge," says the owner. "For me, it's almost a spiritual place."

RIGHT: A cozy sitting area pairs an antique rocking chair with a Burton James armchair and ottoman upholstered in a plaid wool atop a New Moon Mesa wool carpet. The custom-crafted floor lamp is from Misco Mill; the oak side table was formerly a hat stand. The luminous mountain landscape painting is by Swedish-born artist Birger Sandzen, who was a prolific painter and printmaker for more than fifty years until his death in 1954.

FACING: In the efficient kitchen, a white porcelain apron-front sink is set within custom cabinets by Western Millworks. The custom copper sconces are from Stronghold Fabrication. English antique cream jugs, a 1940s-era painting, a wool flat-weave rug by Escalante, and a vintage headboard cabinet add depth and interest to the space. The painting is by American West landscape painter Edgar Payne.

The loft bedroom of the 900-square-foot Buffalo Cabin is lent gravitas through its rich but subdued palette and handcrafted antiques: a Stickley armchair and side table, Pendleton blankets, and Navajo carpets. A vintage hand-painted toy chest adds color and whimsy to the space.

LEFT: Patina adds authenticity and richness to interiors. A vintage milking stool rests on a collectible carpet. The bedside table was converted from an antique dry sink. Custom ticking stripe on the headboards lends a retro feel and pairs well with 1920s-era Native American prints.

ABOVE: A weathered blue bench provides color and a place to set one's hat upon entry to the Moose Cabin. A double-headed hay rake and a colorful, graphic portrait of a Native American woman by Logan Maxwell Hegege—whose contemporary works have a timeless appeal—complete the vignette.

FACING: The serene master bedroom features a collection of cross-stitched samplers from the turn of the last century. Moon wool drapery frames the windows looking out to the west. The vintage brass bed is laid with a hand-loomed bedcover from 1879.

LEFT: In the guest bath, the sink is set within gray Foussana limestone. An antique vessel filled with cattails and a Currier & Ives print of a wild turkey bring nature indoors.

THE ARTFUL CABIN

You know you're in the home of an artist when every object, whether a museum-worthy painting or a repurposed flea-market find, is placed in perfect juxtaposition to the other objects in the rooms. The result is that each item, no matter its value, is elevated to a piece of art. It can be a rarefied experience to visit such a place, where the filled spaces are perfectly balanced by the negative spaces, and where the featured items are positioned in such a way as to create an experience that is at once gallery-like and restorative.

For a pair of artists and art aficionados, their longtime search in Jackson, Wyoming, for a contemporary house suitable for displaying art led them to an unlikely choice: a circa 1989 log home and guest cabin with all the features characteristic of the era. Although the house was well proportioned and in good shape, the varnish applied to the logs decades before had yellowed and become UV-damaged. Inside, an oversized river rock fireplace constituted a domineering presence against floors of Douglas fir and quartzite flagstone. The windows were too small, and the rooms were cut off from one another. Overall, the home was dark and confining, and lacked a healthy connection to the outdoors.

The husband had known John Carney of CLB Architects for a long time. Having purchased the property for its proximity to the ski mountain, the direct view north to the Grand Teton, and its location in a neighborhood in which homes on generous treed lots are screened from the street, he and his wife placed their faith in CLB and Tennyson-Ankeny Construction to enact a dramatic transformation of the structures.

Architect Matt Thackray led the effort and credits the owners—the wife a mixed-media artist, and the husband a wood-turning hobbyist—with being open to ideas and confident enough to challenge the team to think creatively. "Great clients make great projects," he says. "That was the case here."

The house, arrayed on one level with a separate two-bedroom guest cabin, was straightforward in its design. The massive river rock fireplace, "a 700-pound gorilla that overpowered the scale of the living room," according to Thackray, was the first to go, while the yellowed logs were blasted with environmentally friendly ground-up corn cobs and finished to a muted blue-gray on the exterior, where fresh white trim enhanced the newly clean look. Inside, the logs were painted with an alabaster-tinted lacquer. The treatment brightened and united the interiors while also highlighting the texture and cracks in the wood, emphasizing their artistic

The great room of a transformed 1989 log home in Jackson Hole is a study in serenity. The horse race artwork came from a Wyoming bar; when pulled from its frame the effects of decades of tobacco smoke were revealed along its edges. The wood tansu is a Japanese antique, its wheels making it a rare find.

quality. This proved crucial, since the preponderance of true stacked log corners and exposed log ends within the rooms made them very much part of the dialog.

The team covered some log surfaces with dry wall to allow lighting coves and to create a suitable backdrop for art, giving those areas the same alabaster treatment for a smooth transition between surfaces. Circle-sawn Douglas fir floors, whose orange-leaning tone and gapping created a dated, cabin-like feel, were refinished and stained ebony for a modernist contrast. Other significant architectural moves included installing a partial wall between the dining area and kitchen with its breakfast nook, to create a sense of separation without losing openness; reengineering a wall in the art-filled office in order to install a large, room-transforming window; opening up a warren-like series of spaces in the master-bedroom suite; transforming the master bath with floating cabinets, a glass shower, and white subway tile on floors and walls; and introducing generous amounts of glazing in the living room and master bath to take full advantage of the Grand Teton prospect.

Despite the heavy quality of the logs, the home's indoor-outdoor transitions are seamless, with outdoor living spaces created on either side of the house to allow the inhabitants to take advantage of—or escape—the warmth of the sun. Landscape designers Hershberger Design enacted a rustic modern transformation of the landscape contiguous to the house with minimalistic hardscaping and plantings. Rusted Corten steel partitions screen the driveway from the house and define the clean-lined walkways of Peregrine limestone. Terraces edged by tall grasses and lawn amidst mature aspens and cotton-woods give way to meadow spaces extending to the north, where an additional lot was purchased by the owners to safeguard the view.

Inside and out, the house has a light and peaceful feeling, a far cry from the dark and dated ponderousness of its previous incarnation. Carney Logan Burke's Sarah Kennedy worked closely with the owners on conceptualizing the interiors. "These are really creative people who put a lot of thought into the project and weren't afraid to push the boundaries," she explains. "The owner didn't buy art for the house. She just created the most amazing pieces, like a bust covered entirely with pills. She has to take a lot of the credit for its beauty."

With its modest volumes, great light, and perfectly placed objects, the house has a palpable serenity. "It still has that log cabin vibe," says Thackray, "but all around there are modern, crisp rooms that show art well. People want to feel a connection to nature in their homes; this is natural, timeless, and modern all at the same time. It has the cozy qualities of a cabin yet it still feels fresh." And whether the project is a log cabin update or altogether new construction, that is the ultimate goal.

CLB Architects and Tennyson-Ankeny Construction transformed the dated cabin by enlarging openings, painting its yellowed logs with a tinted alabaster lacquer, and coating the orange fir floors with an ebony finish. The Arco floor lamp was designed by Achile and Pier Giacomo Castiglioni for Flos. The newspaper array on the wall was created by the wife, a fine artist.

ABOVE: The office is an art-filled inner sanctum, now bathed in light.

RIGHT: All the wood vessels were made by the husband. Peregrine limestone floors provide a pleasing contrast to the textured white log ends.

Nowhere is the quality of light better appreciated than in the kitchen. There a partial wall was installed to create a sense of separation from the entry and main dining area; the openness comes from an eat-in dining area with built-in window seat and door leading directly to the front patio and garden. Backless counter stools tuck out of sight when not in use. The Moooi tube light echoes the shape and color of the logs. The bust artwork by the owner is covered entirely in white pills.

ABOVE: Master bedroom furniture chosen by the homeowners maintains a low profile and allows the Teton views to take center stage.

FACING ABOVE: In the master bath, a freestanding Victoria and Albert bathtub is centered on a window that was enlarged during the remodel to take in the mountain views. The stools are offcuts from log ends that were removed from the living room when drywall was installed.

FACING BELOW: A secondary bedroom maintains a serene palette of whites.

The cob-blasted logs have a clean appearance appropriate to today's mountain modern ethos. Landscaping by Hershberger Design creates a sense of arrival through a minimal approach using natural grasses, Peregrine limestone walkways, and Corten steel panels.

TIMELESS AUTHENTICITY

I n a home that seems rooted in place, its most telling detail might be the tree trunk that serves as the central post for its spiral staircase. Builder Tim Blazina of Yellowstone Traditions found the windblown lodgepole pine on a friend's property outside his hometown of Red Lodge, Montana. It was strapped on a sledge, dragged out of the woods through the snow, trucked to Jackson Hole, then lifted by crane into the house through a section of the roof that had been left open for just that purpose. Once in place, the debarked and finished tree, flared base and roots still intact, was integrated into the staircase treads and irregular stone slab landing by master craftsmen working on-site. Extending the ethos of bringing nature indoors to its logical conclusion, the tree trunk staircase is just one detail among many in a home that is all about handcraftedness, appropriateness, and authenticity and is uniquely suited to the site.

Architect Peter Zimmerman worked with Yellowstone Traditions, designer Bill Peace, and a host of artisans to create a timeless home in a pristine setting for the Pennsylvania-based owners of the Wilson, Wyoming property. Situated on almost twenty acres surrounded by conservation land at the end of a road, the site enjoys spectacular views through aspens and conifers over protected ranch land to the Tetons and the iconic Sleeping Indian. Working within a proscribed building envelope, a height restriction, and a limitation of less than 4,500 square feet was no hardship for these owners. One of their main goals was that the home feel intimate, with no overscaled rooms, and that the site be as undisturbed as possible, as if it were a meadow naturally appearing in the woodlands. Their success in this pursuit resulted in the project being honored with a Palladio Design Award for traditional architecture.

Structurally, the home is essentially a one-story building with second-level bedrooms tucked under the sloped roof, with generous gabled dormers creating room to breathe and allowing for cozy window seats with far-reaching views. This lent itself to the theme, notes Blazina, as the sloped roof creates the feel of an older house despite the home's substantial size. A separate garage structure is connected by a covered walkway, which lends transparency and allows for a dead-on view of the Sleeping Indian through the breezeway as one approaches the house. Four bedrooms and a bunkroom provide ample berths for holiday gatherings of extended family, while an open kitchen with many handcrafted details offers a highly efficient meal-and party-staging space adjacent to the vaulted great room.

A home in the shadow of the Tetons melds walls of square hand-hewn logs and a cedar-shake roof in a way that feels rooted in place. Designed by architect Peter Zimmerman and built by Yellowstone Traditions, the structure makes the most of its gently sloped site and stunning view of the Sleeping Indian. The project was honored for its thoughtful conception and execution with a Palladio Design Award for traditional architecture.

The entire project is a study in appropriateness. The primary massing employs repeated gabled forms, mimicking the topography of the mountains beyond. The tops of the chimneys were given a crenelated sawtooth treatment, which speaks to the ruggedness of surrounding peaks and boulders while helping them blend into the landscape. On the exterior, antique salvaged, resawn hewn wood was chosen for the natural checking that occurs over time. Naturalistic meadowlike landscaping and organic paths of subtly multicolored stone lead to a plunge pool—concrete lined but made to look natural with rock edges—and a hot tub fashioned to resemble an old wooden rain barrel. The roof of the outdoor living room is supported by tree trunk columns, their bark still visible. An irrigation stream was rerouted closer to the house to further the immersive nature experience.

The owners committed to an interior finished entirely of reclaimed planking and stone—the structure has no exposed drywall or plaster—which creates a warm, textural environment and heightens the sense that the home was built solely from natural materials found on-site. For that reason, square timbers were chosen over round logs, since the area's homesteaders would have been more likely to hew by hand to a square shape. At the base of staircases, organically shaped rocks ground the home and convey the notion they have been built around, as if too heavy to move. In other places, stone fireplaces protrude through walls to the next room to form a bookshelf, or the wall of a shower. European antiques nod to the wife's Irish heritage and mix comfortably with custom forged ironwork, Navajo rugs from the '20s and '30s, and important Western artworks from the homeowners' collection.

"Authenticity was very important to the clients," says designer Bill Peace. "They wanted warmth, comfort, and coziness with a bit of an old-world/new-world feel. Our goal was to make it feel collected-over-time." The result, he says, is a

The form of the structure mimics the mountains beyond, while the crenellated sawtooth treatment on the chimney stacks speaks to the ruggedness of the terrain. The front door, handmade, as is everything else in the home, was crafted of wormy chestnut. A covered connector between house and garage allows for views through to the mountains while approaching the house.

house that's textural rather than merely dark, and that feels like it's been there forever. It will, he adds, age well.

Despite the relatively compact size of the home, Zimmerman was able to incorporate many opportunities for quiet moments in window seats, alcoves with desks, private balconies and sitting rooms, and, the ultimate retreat, an old trapper's cabin. The only building original to the site, it was rebuilt as it was—that is to say, imperfectly non-plumb. Western antiques expert Terry Winchell, owner of Fighting Bear Antiques, was given free rein to fit out the cabin with period-appropriate furnishings and regional relics such as antlers, old horse gear, snowshoes, signage, and vintage hickory chairs. The interior has applied-pole pieces, '30s-era cowboy art, and an old lodgepole pine day bed with a red leather-trimmed cushion. It can handle overflow guests, but its main purpose is as a time-capsule-like retreat from the bustle of the main house.

The entire project, says Zimmerman, was about intimacy, scale, and grounding. "We tried to create an environment almost as if we'd found an old homestead house, then renovated it and added on. It's tied so closely to the land." The result, he continues, is a home that defers to its site, tucked in the woods in the shadow of the Tetons.

The great room is characterized by hand-hewn walls, standing dead log rafters, and a dry-stacked moss rock fireplace. Blacksmith Wil Wilkins made the custom chandelier. "The house was designed to be intimate and at a scale two people could enjoy," says architect Peter Zimmerman, but it also needed to be able to accommodate a crowd. Explains interior designer Bill Peace, who mixed contemporary sofas with period antique chairs, "They wanted a family home where they could come spend time together and have a family experience. They also love to entertain; everyone is welcome all the time."

The owners spend half the year in Wyoming. When their children and grandchildren arrive, there are opportunities for privacy for everyone. The owners' suite includes a lofted area finished with a vintage chair and applied-pole desk leading to a balcony that's perfect for quiet contemplation or a good cigar. A comfortably furnished central upstairs lounge offers the perfect place to read or take a private phone call.

The well-laid-out kitchen has a low ceiling to create a feeling of intimacy and integrated woodwork crafted by Yellowstone Traditions. Cabinets were custom made of wormy chestnut and antique oak; the island slab is walnut and the counter-tops are honed soapstone. The leather-upholstered barstools are from Hickory Chair. Glass-fronted doors lighten the space, while copper pendants from Ann Morris Antiques add a vintage feel.

LEFT: Despite the strictures to stay within a limitation of less than 4,500 square feet, the house has many different spaces for varied uses. The architect used the natural slope of the site to create a sunken lounge with fireplace leading to the patio and hot tub. Traditional-leaning furnishings, such as the custom dining table and chandelier, and a subdued palette imbue the home with a feeling of timelessness.

ABOVE: A dormered volume creates the coziest of guest bedrooms and makes the most efficient use of space.

FACING: In the vaulted master bedroom suite, a classic western-rustic ethos includes exposed log ends in the lofted gallery, a heavy, irregular stone fireplace base, antlers, and traditional art. The graceful iron chandelier is from Rose Tarlow; rug is Edward Fields/Tai Ping. Designer Bill Peace selected suede and Ultrasuede for the headboard and sofa for added comfort and warmth.

LEFT: Light pours into the cozy bunkroom, where the rug and pillows add color and life. Pocket doors can be left open when the room is not in use to enhance the feeling of spaciousness in the home.

BELOW: Rustic meets refined in the graciously scaled master bathroom. The tub has an in-the-treetops feel as well as a view.

ABOVE: The vaulted great room has dynamic architectural elements and is anchored by the irregular stone fireplace, which asserts itself as the heart of the home. Mohair and velvet were used on upholstered pieces for luxury and warmth; the draperies are a de le Cuona Huckleberry Tweed.

FACING: The integration of the monumental stone staircase base into the wood stairs and lodgepole support is a testament to the builder's artistry. Traditional furnishings include Navajo rugs, an antique cabinet from Robuck & Co., and Bill Gollings' 1914 painting *Returning to Camp*.

FACING: Charles Bunney of Yellowstone Traditions built the unique modern steel staircase to the master bedroom loft, creating one of the home's touchstone moments. The tree was a windblown lodgepole pine Tim Blazina found on a friend's property in Montana. The Native American rug and vintage leather chair add color and soften the wood and steel elements.

ABOVE: MD Landscaping reclaimed the site, installing local sandstone patios and native plantings. The hot tub, made to look like an old rain barrel, is a short walk from the patio.

A HOME ON
THE RANGE

For a native western couple living on the East Coast, it was all about the land. Their mission—to find the perfect ranch property, no matter how remote—took them to almost ninety properties scattered across Colorado, Wyoming, Idaho, and Montana. It was the husband who had a lifelong dream of owning a ranch; he had grown up hunting and fishing. It was the wife who undertook the search. The moment she glimpsed the property that would become their ranch, a dramatic site backed by mountains on the edge of Montana's Bob Marshall Wilderness, she knew. "Despite the extreme weather conditions," she recalls, "I fell in love with the openness of the land and how raw and primal it felt."

The topography is stunning: vast open plains that intersect dramatically with timbered limestone escarpments, interspersed with hay meadows. With the reintroduction of bison to the landscape, the ranch hosts every species of animal that was present when Lewis and Clark passed through the region more than 200 years ago. In fact, this relatively pristine part of Montana is one of the last places in the lower 48 where grizzlies still venture out from the mountains onto the plains. While the property is remote, far from a town, ski area, or airport, the couple was more interested in riding, hunting, fishing, and raising their children in nature than logistical convenience or in-town amenities. Long term, they intended to call it home.

Having perused rustic architecture books for years, the landowners were familiar with the work of Pearson Design Group. They knew they wanted a rugged, handmade look appropriate to the region and its history but one that could still be comfortable and livable. When PDG founder Larry Pearson first saw the property, he was awed. "It was powerful. The landscape goes from valley floor to forest peaks, almost like multiple experiences."

The land had been used primarily for cattle ranching for a century; the previous owner had also established it as a recreational fishing outfit. The pastures were overgrazed and the handful of primitive buildings had limited electricity and no telephone access. But wildlife was abundant; even during construction there were signs of bear activity on-site. The task, therefore, explains Pearson, "was more than just producing architecture and design; it was also undertaking an analysis of the ranch and surrounding lands, including wildlife patterns and the effects of wind. The owners took their responsibility very seriously, asking questions like how one can build in a way that is supportive of native landscaping and animal populations."

A home designed by Pearson Design Group and built by On Site Management in close consultation with its owners has a rugged hand-hewn aesthetic appropriate to its remote mountain setting at the edge of Montana's million-plus-acre Bob Marshall Wilderness. It's constructed of restacked walls and trusses of antique hewn timbers, weighty, distinctive chimneys, and a metal roof. The porch columns and rafters are lodgepole pine.

141

The owners undertook a significant amount of habitat restoration work to return riparian corridors to native habitat, and one direct result has been an increase in the moose population. They also made a significant decision early on to ranch with bison rather than cattle. "The ranch was part of the bison's winter range back in the 1800s," says the wife. "Bison grazing habits improve habitat for the various species of birds that depend on the prairie, and bison are complementary to the grass range, as long as you can keep them moving. They are also largely impervious to the extreme weather changes you have on the front."

First, though, the owners needed a working compound. Architecturally, they sought an updated rustic aesthetic in structures built to last. To this end, On Site Management was a crucial partner, contributing fine craftsmanship, meticulous attention to detail, and creative problem-solving, an important consideration when one is fifty minutes from the nearest town and dealing with Montana weather. The team—homeowners, architects, and contractors (the owners did their own interior design in partnership with PDG)—worked on the plans for close to four years, from siting the access road to building in multiple phases. The ranch manager's house came first, followed by other ranch outbuildings—ultimately twelve structures in all. For a full year, the owners lived on-site in a yurt.

"We were asked to reinvent the ranch in a historic but nouveau way," says PDG lead architect Justin Tollefson. All structures had to have an eye on history but also needed to meet a young rancher's needs. There would be a working compound which would serve as the hub of activities, with various support buildings and a caretaker's house. There would also be a main lodge for the owners, a romantic getaway cabin for guests, and a classic barn designed as an iconic marker in the landscape.

The two-story main house is sited in a protected valley in an old mule pasture. It is constructed of restacked walls and trusses of antique hewn timbers and grounded by weighty, distinctive fireplaces, with lodgepole pine porches and rafters, reclaimed plank exterior siding, and a metal roof. Interiors are finished with reclaimed hemlock interior paneling and flooring and, in the kitchen, antique white oak and reclaimed hemlock cabinetry. The emphasis is on regional appropriateness and handmade integrity. "It's a functioning home and ranch as much as it is a retreat," Tollefson explains. "We attempted to create something that represents the material palette of the American ranch."

The owners came to the project having done an enormous amount of research. The wife had assembled a voluminous, pre-Pinterest design brief, an assemblage of inspiration

The homeowners scouted almost ninety properties throughout the mountain West to find the perfect site to build a ranch from the ground up. The project consisted of twelve structures, starting with a working compound and including a main house, guest house, and iconic barn. What used to be cattle pasture now supports bison, a species that can withstand tough conditions while walking softly on the land.

photos with descriptions, even detailing preferred masonry style and finishes. They had well-thought-out ideas regarding what they were seeking, she says. "We wanted a home; we didn't want a lodge. And we wanted it to look as though it had been there a hundred years but with a little touch of Gstaad, with fur blankets and modern furniture."

All furniture, textiles, and artwork choices were driven by the owners. They worked closely with blacksmith Wil Wilkins, for example, to design authentic handcrafted accents using repurposed materials such as wagon wheels, barbed wire, and ore-cart track. These touches extended to the great room chandelier and sconces, as well as cabinet hardware and mudroom hooks. They scoured sources across the country to create clean interiors which combine antiques, traditional artwork, antlers, and wildlife mounts with contemporary, comfortable furnishings.

As it is a working ranch, the work continues. A recent addition is a separate outbuilding linked to the house by a glass connector. As always when building in a pristine area on the edge of a major wilderness area, sensitivity to site remains paramount. For the owners, it's about respecting the environment—the land, vegetation, wildlife, regional history, and neighbors. It's also about being self-reliant when far from town and subject to long, harsh winters. Special places demand an attitude of stewardship and thoughtful consideration in animals to graze; deciding where to build and how to fence to mitigate effects on wildlife and neighbors; and considering the aesthetics of new construction in a timeless landscape.

This new old ranch was built to sit lightly on the land while lasting for generations. And as exemplified by the roaming bison, now thriving, it embraces the past while looking to the future.

BELOW: A Tibetan prayer horn lies on a petrified redwood slab atop a base by blacksmith Wil Wilkins. Custom crystal-and-bronze lighting fixture is by Ochre; handblown ice sconces by Lianne Gold through Ralph Pucci.

RIGHT: Pollaro redwood slab coffee table, Alexander Lamont leather chairs and candlesticks, BDDW couches and chairs ground the lodgelike great room. Wil Wilkins made fireplace tools, chandeliers, sconces and door hardware. The zebra ottoman and organic side table bring the outdoors in.

ABOVE: A mudroom entry has room for boots, cowboy hats, slickers, and all the tools of the ranching trade. It also has an English signal cannon and antique Ethiopian chairs. The hammered-iron sconces, sourced from Patrick Kovacs Kunsthandel, were part of a hunting room presented at the 1910 International Hunting Exhibition in Vienna.

RIGHT: A quiet office with an English partner's desk is illuminated by 19th-century brass chandeliers from Denton Antiques in London. The distinctive fireplace is a Pearson Design Group specialty. Western art—Julius Seyler's *Blackfoot Indian* and Carl Rungius's *Goats*—completes the tableau.

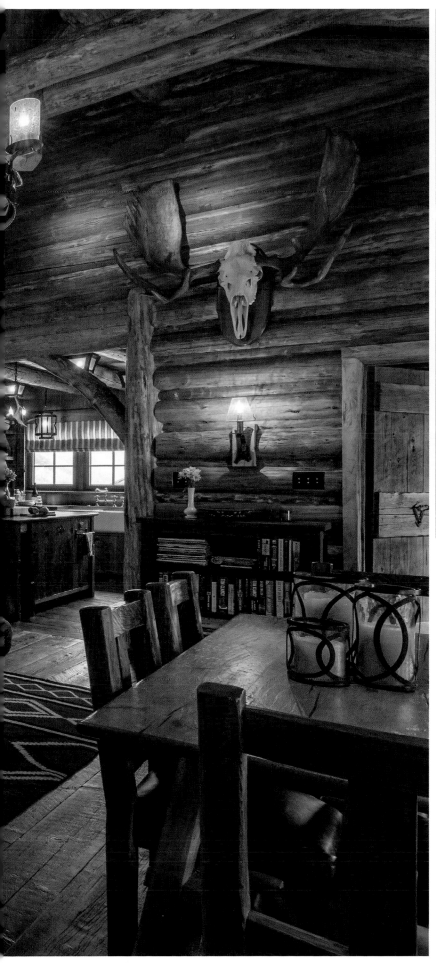

LEFT: The guesthouse living area has the feel of a full-size home with a kitchen, dining area, and living room with a stone fireplace. Wil Wilkins made the chandelier and fireplace screen and tools. The dining table and chairs were handcrafted by On Site Management. Comfortable furniture and built-in window seats lend a homey feel.

ABOVE: An apron-front sink, beamed ceiling, and generous island make for efficient meal prep in a welcoming space.

FACING: The homeowners spend a lot of time in the cozy sitting area situated between the kitchen and dining room; its asymmetrical fireplace exudes warmth and charm. The Moroccan carpet is antique, from Doris Leslie Blau. The remarkable side table is an Indonesian lychee wood stump from Balsamo.

ABOVE: In the kitchen of the main house, tile from Paris Ceramics is combined with Taj Mahal quartzite countertops and custom-made oak cabinets by On Site Management. Lighting fixtures are antique; the oven hood and pot rack were handmade by Bill Moore of Bar Mill Iron Forge. Brass mugs are from BDDW.

The graciously proportioned master bedroom is illuminated by an antique brass chandelier and sconces from Bjorn Wiinblad. The Bronze/Holly cabinet, nightstands, and walnut slab headboard are from BDDW. The rugs are Turkish. Art photography by Nick Brandt bring the wild indoors.

FACING: A custom copper and tin tub from William Holland occupies pride of place in the master bath; perched nearby is the Pieds de Bouc stool by Marc Bankowsky. The pendant is vintage Austrian.

LEFT: An early 1900s tramp art mirror flanked by antique 19th-century railroad sconces found on 1st Dibs hangs over an applied-pole vanity made by the woodworkers at On Site Management.

ABOVE: The new owners did extensive amounts of land and riparian habitat restoration on the property, which was formerly a working cattle ranch. The property is within prime grizzly bear habitat.

RIGHT: An iconic barn serves as a marker in the landscape. Classic in form, it is built to last with reclaimed wood, a fire-savvy standing-seam metal roof, shed roofs, and double cupolas.

WINE COUNTRY CLASSIC

Laura Parker had already spent a lifetime in the advertising business when she embarked on a dramatic career reboot. It was buying her first home in Del Mar, California, that changed the trajectory of her life so abruptly. She had hired a contractor to renovate that house and in working with him discovered that she loved the renovation process. She was so exhilarated by it, in fact, that she ended up buying, remodeling, and selling four more houses. It was during the course of those projects that she realized she was burnt out on advertising; she had grown up in the business (her father ran a large advertising firm), pursued it straight out of college, and even founded her own successful agency. Yet ever since the day her contractor said, "You can't do what I do," Parker determined to prove him wrong. Over the next eighteen years, Parker's Del Mar Restoration built or remodeled more than fifty beautifully designed, carefully constructed, environmentally conscious Southern California homes.

Female contractors are scarce, Parker allows, but for her it was a relatively seamless transition. "It's really not that different from advertising," she says. "You have clients, a timeline, and a creative process. It was easy for me to be a contractor, and a good one, because I have more of a professional background than most contractors."

With her second career established, life was rewarding, but Parker yearned for a rural experience. She had grown up visiting a family friend on a vineyard in upstate New York, and even at a young age she internalized the appeal of the lifestyle. She began taking trips to Napa Valley and scouting around until she stumbled across the perfect project: a two-acre property in the Oak Knoll district with three vintage buildings and a working vineyard. She calls it "the perfect canvas to renovate in an authentic vernacular." It even came with a bright yellow 1969 Ford pickup.

The three buildings—a turn-of-the-century farmhouse, a small 1930s barn, and a Sear's kit cottage from the 1950s, all in need of a loving update—were clustered together on the property, leaving most of the acreage available for vines. Over a five-year period, Parker completely renovated and restored the existing buildings. The compound now consists of a three-bedroom, three-bath main house with pool; a three-bedroom, two-and-a-half-bath barn with a wine-tasting room, and a one-bedroom, one-bath cottage. At one point in the process, Parker took a seven-month hiatus from work to live on the property and study leatherwork with

A collection of vintage buildings with a working vineyard in the California wine country were made complete by the addition of a traditional post-and-beam barn. Contractor Laura Parker bought the 22 x 24 foot barn with an added dormer as a kit from Country Carpenters, oversaw the construction herself, and then had it painted in Valspar Barn Red. The weather in Napa Valley allows for alfresco dining year-round. Parker's table is watched over by an antique metal deer head found at Solo, in Solana Beach, California.

ABOVE: The homeowner bought a derelict 1880s barn across the valley and used its 2-inch-thick Douglas fir boards for the renovation of the property's original barn. Leftover boards were used to build Parker's custom-made cantilevered desk. Vintage signs are from Parker's sister's store, Sister Salvage, in upstate New York.

FACING ABOVE: The counter with shelving dividing the main living space was made from salvaged barnwood and galvanized siding.

FACING BELOW: An Alape wall-mounted work sink makes a simple sculptural statement.

a woman who had made bags for Hermes. The only thing missing now was a leathercraft workshop—ideally housed within the iconic red barn of her childhood dreams.

Parker envisioned a big-beamed mortise-and-tenon structure, but after five years of renovation in Napa and still running her own contracting business in southern California, she had no desire to undertake a project on that scale (which would typically involve locating an existing mortise-and-tenon barn, disassembling it, moving it, and rebuilding it). There was another option, though: building a barn from a kit. She worked with an architect to determine the most appropriate scale and placement; they decided a 22- by 24-foot, one-and-a-half story barn would be ideal. Fortuitously, after researching and identifying her preferred kit company, she found that the Connecticut-based Country Carpenters offered a barn with those exact specifications. It wasn't long before an 18-wheeler loaded with 400 precut and numbered pieces rolled up amidst the vines. Although Parker had to retain an engineer to retrofit the structure to meet California earthquake codes (extra hold-downs to secure the structure to the foundation and additional metal straps hidden within the mortise-and-tenon joints) and a crane to hoist the big beams into place, the barn raising took only a few weeks.

Ever the practical contractor, Parker knew that in order to work there she needed year-round comfort and functionality. She designed the barn with five inches of insulation, which necessitated buying two packages of siding and extending the rafters nine inches. The final step was painting it the perfect shade, Valspar Barn Red.

This quintessentially American structure—with its cross gables, cupola, and vibrant color—houses Parker's leather workshop, serves as a party-staging area, and offers an upstairs "napping quarters," lounge space, and bathroom. Throughout the interiors, as in all the compound's buildings, the look is clean, timeless, and rustic, and is replete with vintage finds like painted signs and repurposed pieces, such as a shower made from a round metal horse trough and an old French washbasin used as a sink.

In the course of remodeling the property's original barn, Parker had purchased an 1800s barn from the opposite side of the Napa Valley. Its two-inch-thick Douglas fir boards were used throughout that renovation, and there was enough left over for her to add special touches to the new structure: countertops and a cantilevered desk downstairs, floating nightstands, and sliding doors upstairs. She also used the barnwood to construct a multipurpose table, which she mounted on red casters from a local antique shop. The concrete floor, practical, efficient, and cool in the summer, is warmed by throw rugs, while tactile details include heavy-duty hand-forged plumbing fixtures.

Parker spends as much time as possible in Napa, often arriving with a large group of friends and her constant companion, Earl, a yellow Labrador. Ultimately, her retirement vision involves doing leatherwork at her desk of reclaimed wood in the big red barn amongst the vineyards. In the meantime, the barn, although the newest structure on the historic property, is already the property's most iconic landmark. "It really does look like it's been there for 100 years," she says. "And that's been my philosophy in everything I do—to build homes to look like they've been there 100 years, and to build them to last that long as well."

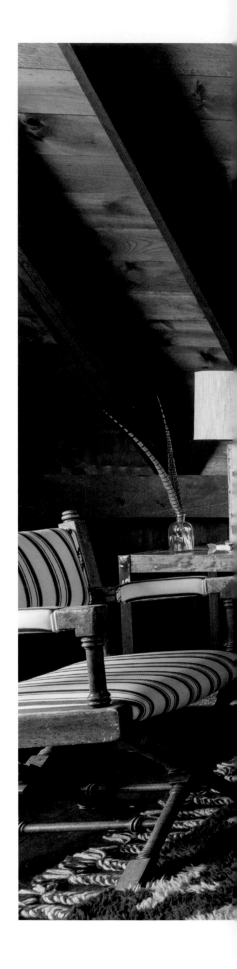

The second floor is home to a lounging nook with a distressed leather sofa from Restoration Hardware, a cross rug from Anthropologie, and a table with a wool-rug top and crates underneath procured from the Alameda Swap Meet.

LEFT: In the bathroom, the locally sourced galvanized sink sits atop a barnwood counter and cabinet.

RIGHT: The whimsical shower is actually a horse trough, found nearby at the Wilson Feed Store. The plumbing fixtures are from Sonoma Forge.

FACING: A quiet napping spot features a sturdy oak bed, an old Hudson's Bay blanket, and Schoolhouse Electric sconces. The nightstands were made from salvaged barnwood.

LOG CABIN HOLIDAY

Nothing says "Welcome home for the holidays" more cheerfully than a log cabin, with its interior glowing, its front door draped with an evergreen garland and framed by lanterns while thick snowflakes fall from above. For the new owners of a home in Alta, Wyoming, this Norman Rockwellian picture was not at all what they'd envisioned for themselves. But that fact does little to detract from its appeal now. There's a reason this enduring style feels like home.

The couple had been living in the Grand Targhee area for some years and had planned to build a new home in a rustic modern style with light-filled contemporary interiors. But then they saw a four-bedroom log home on a ten-acre property that had no visible neighbors. With mountain views, mature trees, a live creek, and space for a barn, guesthouse, and ponds, it exemplified rural peace.

The homeowners needed a place that was cozy for two but could easily expand to accommodate additional numbers. And because they're avid travelers who follow global designs and trends, they were interested in a more contemporary aesthetic. "It was the property that spoke to us," recalls the owner. "We had zero interest in a log home. We felt it was too much wood, was too rustic, and would require too much maintenance." Longtime acquaintances of Rush Jenkins and Klaus Baer of WRJ Design, they asked the designers to take a look at the house, wondering whether, despite the logs, it would be possible to create a modern and contemporary feel. The designers were enthusiastic, pointing to the strong bones of the house, its open floor plan, and its beautiful river rock fireplace.

Rush Jenkins says he enjoys the log-home challenge. The main question is always how to move the house toward the light, which means working against the logs' heavy, dark propensity. The orange hue of the standard log homes from the 1980s now looks dated, he adds, so changing the tones is crucial. His first move in these cases is to stain the floors to gray or middle brown tones and bring the aesthetic of a lighter color palette, typically grays and blues. This is not as invasive or expensive as changing the color of the logs themselves (which is possible, as cumbersome and expensive as it is), yet can achieve close to the same effect.

Once the home's overall palette was refined, the front door was replaced and the entryway made brighter and grander. The kitchen was redesigned and the bathrooms updated. Drywall was repainted from a

A dated 1990s-era log cabin was the last thing the owners envisioned for themselves in a new home. Rather, they had in mind one that was light-filled and rustic modern in style. But after finding the perfect property in Alta, Wyoming, and bringing in Vera Iconica Architecture and WRJ Design to update the structure, they became log-home converts due to the form's charm, solidity, and appropriateness and for its enduring appeal in a Rocky Mountain setting.

FACING: The purchasers of a home on the Idaho side of the Wyoming Tetons hired WRJ Design to renovate their log cabin in time for the holidays. The new front door, designed by WRJ, transforms a traditional entry. The designers added interest through the addition of fur pillows on a Poltrona Frau woven-leather bench and the Visual Comfort Cubist chandelier in aged iron and glass.

LEFT: A shell-fronted cabinet adds a touch of brightness and a decided glam factor to the master bedroom, while the mirror invites light into log-walled interiors.

yellow tone to a creamy white, while the floors were refinished. The new dark grayish hue created a strong contrast to the walls and made the white chinking pop. Strong, rustic western statement items like elk antler chandeliers were replaced with cleaner, lighter, and more modern fixtures, which went a long way toward transforming the ambience. A bar and wine refrigerator were installed for effortless, more welcoming entertaining. A stylish and functional mudroom was added to accommodate all the necessary accessories for the homeowners' favorite outdoor pursuits, such as skiing, biking, and fly-fishing. Sumptuous fabrics were introduced throughout in cream, gray, white, and blue tones to create a quiet backdrop for carefully curated contemporary art pieces.

Jenkins and his colleague Sabrina Schreibeis oversaw the transformation, with WRJ's Amanda Jordan helping with the holiday styling for the couple's first Christmas in the new-old home. First they selected a color palette that harmonizes with the room. The combination of white, silver, and crystal references the snow on the nearby Teton peaks while creating a sophisticated fairyland feel. Then they sought to engage all the senses. Luxurious textures like sheepskin throws and woven blankets in rich jewel tones added coziness and warmth, providing a contrast to sleek metallic items. White lilies mixed with cedar boughs contributed seasonal scents and established a connection to nature. In an original variation on the tried and true, they incorporated baby's breath into the classic evergreen boughs on the mantel, which introduced texture and scent while having a softening effect. The tabletop at the center of the festivities was deliberately kept simple and elegant, with antler candleholders, uncomplicated place settings, and a variety of candles to foster an intimate conviviality for those gathered around the table.

In the heart of winter, when darkness falls early and the valley is covered with snow, the dwelling glows with seasonal spirit. It is then that the charm of the transformation is most fully appreciated by its new owners. Early in the process, the wife recalls, they had envisioned a structure of stone and reclaimed lumber with steel windows. What they ended up with was almost the complete opposite. To the homeowners' surprise, the resulting rooms enjoy the warmth of logs and the aura of a mountain home, yet feel current and sophisticated.

For Jenkins, every log saved, every home reconfigured for today, brings great satisfaction as a move toward more sustainable living. "Log homes are really wonderful," he says. "And kind of like restoring old cars, once you go in and redo the components they can be really beautiful as well."

A mix of textures and luxurious fabrics, such as Loro Piana drapes, creates cozy, inviting interiors. Says WRJ Senior Designer Sabrina Schriebes, "We like to use neutrals and add texture with furs, wools, linens, and natural fibers."

FACING: The Belgian dining table, with a bluestone top and fumed teak legs, is overhung by a chandelier from the owner's collection. Wool upholstered chairs were made in the US; rug is a mosaic mix of cowhides from Brazil. A holiday palette of green, white, and glass creates a simple and elegant tabletop.

ABOVE: The kitchen and butler's pantry achieve a sense of airiness with glass-fronted cabinets, Taj Mahal quartzite countertops, smoked-glass pendants, and a light palette juxtaposed against dark floors. WRJ reupholstered existing counter chairs to match the drapes.

ABOVE: White caulking between the logs and furniture with slim-pro-file legs help lighten the home's mass. The introduction of natural materials through the wicker basket and wood trough with pine cones adds texture.

FACING: Seasonal greenery and a river rock fireplace create an invit-ing backdrop for a pair of luxurious chairs with leather armrests, linen upholstery, and fur pillows. The custom coffee table was designed by WRJ and made by Packsaddle Road. The artwork is by abstract painter Bradford Stewart.

SPIRITED SKI HOME

Rain Houser and Skye Anderson thrive on being involved in designing a home from its inception, especially when they can participate in conceptualizing the interior layout and hard furnishings. But the founders of Urbaine Home in Bozeman also love the challenge inherent in working within an existing template built to a high standard for contemporary mountain living. In such a case there's a joyful mandate: to personalize a space to reflect the lives of the owners in ways that are spiritedly unique—and to transform a space into a home.

A 5,500-square-foot townhouse at the Yellowstone Club in Big Sky, Montana, was designed by architect Andrew Brechbuhler as part of a compound of sophisticated high-country homes. The dwellings would be traditional in style, but would lean modern in the interiors to create a fresh, clean, mountain-appropriate palette that homeowners could make their own. When designing, Brechbuhler says, he tries to keep the forms simple, clean, and in proportion so that spaces are nicely scaled, have good flow for active families and for entertaining, and offer a pleasing sense of progression. In these high-elevation locales, in addition to addressing challenging topography, heavy snow load, and possible site instability, he prioritizes maximizing views and creating usable exterior spaces—protected areas that can be enjoyed even in winter.

The entry from the street to the three-level home makes an immediate statement in the use of steel on the staircase and its choice of wall treatments: a combination of reclaimed barnboard on ceilings, trim, and select walls, and neutral painted surfaces contrasted with stone. The effect is striking immediately upon entry to the low-ceilinged foyer. There, Houser and Anderson created a jewel-box effect through the installation of an eye-catching custom-made bronze console. Built by designer and artisan Tim Sanford of Bozeman, the console has a contemporary finish but reflects the transitional rustic modern look with the introduction of a wood-grain pattern on its facade. A textured, earth-toned runner and an artistic array of vintage rattan mirrors sourced internationally set against a multihued stone wall complete the effect.

From the entry one is drawn by the view and sense of space to the great room where the volume opens up dramatically. The living room, with its high, sloped, wood-beamed ceiling and glass end wall facing the mountain prospect, opens to an outdoor deck with additional seating. The adjacent kitchen and dining area are tucked under a lower ceiling to create a sense of intimacy and separation within the open plan. The top floor is

In a Yellowstone Club townhouse designed by architect Andrew Brechbuhler, Rain Houser and Skye Anderson of Urbaine Home worked with the owners to pursue the mandate of "fun and young." The curved lines of the caribou-hide-covered chairs and the sleek grid of the metal firewood box add a contemporary contrast to traditional wood and stone elements. The elk mount over the fireplace is by Kirsten Kainz, and the gold-leaf ram skull on the coffee table is by Owen Mortensen. Interwoven porcelain antlers redefine the classic antler chandelier.

given over to the master-bedroom suite, which faces the view, and a quiet study, while the expansive lower level accommodates three bedrooms and a large rec room with bar.

At the time of purchase, the owners had three children under the age of seven. They envisioned family-friendly interiors that were youthful and fun; they didn't want anything too precious or fragile. The pursuit of elegance and comfort with durability allowed for sumptuous alpaca draperies, sheepskin rugs, and sturdy but beautiful furniture in luxurious fabrics and leather. A dusky blue runs throughout the house, appearing in upholstery, drapes, counter chairs, and the powder room vanity; it ties the interiors together while referencing the sky. Throughout the home, statement lighting defines the spaces: a wreath of interwoven porcelain antlers in the living room; soap-bubble pendants in the dining room; a Bocci chandelier in the master bedroom; and, suspended over the kitchen island, handmade glass pendants by Montana artisan Ona Magaro. Elements of surprise abound in such details as a hair-on-hide headboard and a side table made from a stump sheathed in leather in the master bedroom; a sculptural lacquered polar bear bookshelf in the bunkroom; and an urban-edge wallpaper behind the bar in which the words "Kiss Me" have the trompe l'oeil effect of a neon sign.

A sleek steel box for firewood injects a modern sculptural presence in the living room, while the powder room marries a bold wallpaper featuring an oversized bull's-eye target with vintage mirrors and a custom-made vintage-look arrow that lights up. Many original interpretations—such as a living-room end table made from a stump encased in resin, and a coat-closet niche with hair-on-hide walls—combine mountain and modern in a fresh way. References to nature appear throughout the home, from Pendleton fabric deer mounts to curtains with velvet deer heads to the ethereal chandelier in the nursery, an assemblage of more than 100 white butterflies. Straight-from-nature touches, such as sheepskin, hair-on-hide, and fur, appear throughout the house: on furniture, in throws, on the floors—even lining the inside of the bunk bed niches.

The effect is lively and playful. It offers original and unexpected interpretations yet is still elegant and comfortable—a ski house imperative. "They wanted it to feel like a mountain house," explains Houser, "but they still wanted it to be clean and bright. We always focus on bringing warmth through texture. But as with the simple stone fireplace against the white wall, this house really is about simplicity, along with natural materials and fun art."

The art is anything but staid. The designers worked with the owners to choose paintings by Amy Ringholz, Bill Schenck, Tracy Stuckey, and a series of whimsical wildlife photographs by Nine Francois. In yet another indication that this is not your typical '80s mountain home, the elk mount occupying the traditional pride-of-place over the fireplace mantel is a Kirsten Kainz art piece made entirely of found objects. It's just one more detail that advances the mandate "fun and young" for a family with flair.

On the lower level, a wet bar with a built-in refrigerator anchors one end of a lounging space. The trompe l'oeil effect Wall & Decò wallpaper was procured through Urbaine Home. The table lamp is vintage.

RIGHT: In the dining room, a bold painting by Tracy Stuckey celebrates the contemporary West. The hair-on-hide rug is from Kyle Bunting. The leather bench is a vintage gymnasium piece.

FACING: The main-level great room and outdoor dining space take full advantage of expansive mountain views. Lower ceilings over the kitchen and dining areas create intimacy within the larger volume. Statement lighting throughout the house includes handmade glass pendants by Montana artisan Ona Magaro.

FACING: The entry hall makes a statement to new arrivals with a bronze art piece console by Tim Sanford of Bozeman. An array of vintage rattan mirrors, brass candlesticks from Alexander Lamont, and a collectible tramp art box complete the vignette.

LEFT: The textural wood walls, ceiling, and Kyle Bunting hair-on-hide headboard are balanced by the ethereal grace of a Bocci bubble cluster chandelier. The sheepskin stool is from Azadeh Shladovsky; the Baxter lounge chairs are available through Urbaine Home in Bozeman.

RIGHT: The powder room wows with its custom target wallpaper from Wall & Decò, an antique round mirror, and a custom arrow sconce.

FACING: A comfortable and convivial wood-walled rec room is grounded by a Verellen sofa in Holland & Sherry wool plaid fabric atop a sheepskin rug. Wildlife photography by artist Nine Francois adds a playful element, as does the Bambi stool, available through Urbaine Home.

FACING: A soft, light, inviting effect was achieved in the nursery with a Wall & Decò wallpaper of a deer in snow, a fluffy rug, a white crib, and an uber comfortable Ligne Roset Togo fireside chair. A chandelier made from more than a hundred white butterflies floats above.

LEFT: Custom-designed bunks lined in shearling accommodate extra numbers in the utmost comfort. The whimsical Polar Bear Bookcase is available through Urbaine Home.

LAKESIDE CABIN STYLE

Deep within a hardwood forest in rural Tennessee lies a hidden spring-fed lake. The place has a wild hush and ethereal beauty about it, one that is only enhanced by the building that seems to hover above its surface near the shoreline. At once graceful yet grounded, fanciful yet weighty, the structure, with its arched stone supports, angled bracing, and overhanging rusted roof with cupola, integrates into its site in a way that is both novel and harmonious.

The design has an unlikely backstory going back half a century to when the owner, Lee Beaman, was a kid on a six-week family road trip through the American and Canadian West. When they reached the Tetons, Beaman recalls, he was so taken with the spectacular mountain scenery he convinced his parents to stay for a week. He has returned regularly ever since, owning homes in Wyoming and Colorado in the process. In the course of his time in Wyoming, he visited a house that was so of the land, and that so perfectly handled the indoor-outdoor nexus, he was struck. "It really brought the outside indoors, and made you feel you were part of the land," he says. When his dream of finding a private lake near his Nashville home came to fruition, he knew which architect he would call.

It didn't take Paul Bertelli and Logan Leachman of JLF Architects and Design Builders long to realize the extraordinary opportunity the project represented. The owner had scoured topographic maps and realtor listings for years to find the site: a 400-acre parcel an hour from Nashville with a 50-acre private lake at its center. Having owned a home on a government-controlled lake, Beaman had been frustrated by the restrictions and sought a place where he could have a dock right near the house. He also was interested in a lake with clear water, not easy to find in Tennessee during the high heat of summer, that he could reach without battling traffic. The owner of the property had been planning to subdivide after creating the lake, but Beaman successfully negotiated to buy the entire property.

JLF Architects, along with its design-build partner Big-D Construction in Salt Lake City, built the caretaker's house first, envisioning it as a gatehouse through which one drives to access the property. The road meanders through woods and meadows for almost a mile, yielding occasional tantalizing glimpses of the lake as one approaches the house, and terminates at a circular drive on the uphill side of the compoundlike home. There, the lake reveals itself in stages, first through a glass-walled connector between two of the

Homeowner Lee Beaman searched for years to find the perfect site for a lakeside home outside Nashville. He found it on a 400-acre property with a private 50-acre spring-fed lake at its center, then retained JLF Architects and Design Builders to design a one-of-a-kind structure that would make the most of lakeside living. The result, he says, "looks like it belongs there."

masses, and then, once inside, through generous windows and glassed-in areas that link the structures.

Originally conceived as the guesthouse, then expanded slightly to become the main house, the four discrete parts relate to each other and the lake in a way that is more organic and less domineering than might have resulted from other approaches. At one end, near the boat dock, storage shed, and naturalistically hardscaped swimming pool, a self-contained structure hosts three guest bedrooms with their own unimpeded views of the water. The other end of the compound is anchored by the master-bedroom suite, which faces north over the lake (in contrast to the guesthouse's western orientation) and enjoys a private limestone terrace with fire pit at water's edge. At the center lies the main living area, from which a glass-walled bridge accesses the porch.

The grace and presence of the floating porch structure belies the hours of research that went into its design. Many discussions centered on how exactly to build it the way the architects envisioned. Regulations prohibited draining the lake or creating a coffer dam, while lowering the lake level then raising it afterward would have meant a year of exposed banks. Leachman headed the effort to find a solution, ultimately proposing the winning approach: drive steel piles into the lake bed using a barge-based crane, then place precast stone-faced concrete sleeves over them. Both within and without, the building has both gravitas and grace. Usable in all seasons (thanks to interchangeable screens and windows and the introduction of heat), the room can be enjoyed in all weather, for reading, entertaining, or watching the myriad waterfowl that take refuge on the lake.

From porch to living room to bedrooms, the material palette is consistent, unifying the forms with exteriors of reclaimed siding and timbers, stacked limestone walls, and overhanging rusted

Corten steel roofs. Cupolas and stacked stone chimneys add visual interest to the rooflines. The interiors are defined by doors, flooring, and timbers of richly hued reclaimed chestnut sourced from a dilapidated barn the architecture team located and purchased near the Tennessee-Kentucky border. In furnishings, Beaman was seeking comfort and a timeless appeal. This was achieved with the help of designers Roger Higgins and Ann Shipp, who decorated the rooms with antiques, hooked rugs, flea-market finds, and comfortable leather-and-chenille-upholstered furniture.

The compound has a palpable, time-standing-still quality. When you enter the property, notes Leachman, "you feel like you've left it all behind. You don't see any other structures or power lines—nothing." Then you reach the house and contemplate the porch element as it appears to float over the surface of the water. The grounded strength lent by the stone base balances with the cantilevered floor and overhanging roof, which serves both a practical purpose as protection from sun and rain, as well as an aesthetic one. "From the heavy base to the roofline the effect is delicate yet substantial," says Leachman. "We wanted it to look like it wasn't going anywhere." In that they were successful. The home not only looks as though it has always been there, as Lee Beaman notes, "It looks like it belongs."

Struck by the strong sense of place exhibited in a Wyoming residence designed by JLF Architects, Beaman recruited the Montana-based firm and its design-build partner Big-D Construction to design his home in Tennessee. "I really liked the idea of architect and contractor working hand in hand," he says. Sited in multiple components linked by glass connectors and limestone patios along the edge of the private lake, the home makes the most of its water's-edge placement while blending with the landscape rather than dominating it.

The home, built with reclaimed wood and timbers, stacked limestone and Corten steel, roofs with cupolas, and stacked chimneys is comprised of four main components: three guest bedrooms on one side facing west over the water; the master bedroom suite facing north on the opposite end of the compound; the living area in a larger central structure; and a distinctive floating porch where the stone base, explains JLF project manager and architect Logan Leachman, gives it a "grounded strength."

FACING: The interiors are characterized by richly hued chestnut boards used for the floors, doors, and timbers. The wood came from a dilapidated barn near the Tennessee-Kentucky border.

ABOVE: The homeowner and designers Roger Higgins and Ann Shipp sourced antiques, hooked rugs, and found items to lend a sense of history while also upholstering furniture in textural fabrics and leather for comfort and durability. The large oil painting is by Chris Reilly.

RIGHT: An antique daybed provides the perfect fall-asleep-while-reading spot. Antiques like the Dutch chairs around the dining table give the lakeside camp a feel of timelessness.

FACING: The vaulted-ceiling porch, accessed by a glass and timber bridge, extends over the water. Protective overhangs shield the room from the heat of the southern sun in the winter, while screen panels allow the air to flow freely, aided by vintage-looking fans. In the winter the screens can be swapped out for glass and the heat turned on for year-round comfort. Palecek ottomans provide extra seating yet can be tucked out of the way when not in use.

FACING: An efficient kitchen keeps everything within reach. The custom cabinets, made of beech by Big-D Construction in Salt Lake City, set against the darker chestnut floors impart a light and airy feel.

ABOVE: In a simple bed and bathroom with a clean design, an antique brass bed and vintage textiles convey a country charm.

"In the winter, it feels warm and inviting with the fireplaces," says the owner. He wanted to decorate with old pieces, many of which were found at flea markets. "If we wanted the house to feel like it was old," he explains, "the furnishings needed to look old and fit right in."

Local builder James Humphrey dug the 55-foot-deep lake and unearthed the rocks and boulders used around the property. Natural landscaping helps the buildings integrate into their site on the edge of a hardwood forest. The property attracts a multitude of wildlife and birds species, including bald eagles.

MINIMALIST
FISHING RETREAT

Destination holiday towns throughout the Mountain West are riddled with what were, in the 1980s and 1990s, the aspirational standard: high-end log homes. These blown-up versions of the universally iconic mountain structure are defined by exposed logs inside and out, true stacked corners, vaulted-ceilinged great rooms, and river rock fireplaces. Sadly, they are also defined by their yellow-brown hue, their big inefficient volumes, and their generally poor energy ratings. Although usually sturdily built and often constructed of hand-hewn logs by dedicated artisan builders, these plus-sized cabins, while possessing a certain timeless appeal, are now not only dated but unable to meet the demands of a contemporary lifestyle.

When Eric Logan of CLB Architects was shown the house his new client had purchased, he knew he had a project ahead of him. Its prospect was extraordinary, but the structure was a poorly conceived and shoddily constructed iteration of the 1990s ideal. The client, a passionate fly-fisherman and outdoorsman who intended to use the house primarily in the summer, had fallen for the site. Located just five minutes from the town of Jackson, Wyoming, the ten-acre property has lush, open meadows, mature cottonwoods that lend a feeling of privacy, a dramatic butte with a rock face that plunges right down to the edge of the site, and dead-on north-facing views of the Tetons. It also abuts the conservation property held in common by the development—large ponds that are protected habitat for swans and other birds. Best of all, it has an idyllic spring creek flowing right past the view side of the house.

This slice of paradise was marred by its architecture, which, though marginally habitable, begged for a thorough renovation. Not only was the house—three gabled forms with steep pitched roofs—poorly planned and haphazardly massed, it was structurally unsound. According to Jake Ankeny of Ankeny Construction Management, its logs weren't properly pinned to each other or anchored to the foundation. The structure had settled and nothing was level. The couple authorized Logan and Ankeny, whose team was ably led by site superintendent Gary Zundel, to start drawing up plans and estimates and to work with both the county and the homeowners' association to determine what could be done within existing structural regulations and aesthetic guidelines. A radical renovation, much of it constructed with the existing logs, was enacted upon the original foundation. The result is a sleek, modern expression of the contemporary West.

CLB Architects were tasked with reimagining a dated 1990s log home on 10 acres in Jackson, Wyoming. A total rebuild was not an option due to its proximity to a fishing stream, so the architects kept the basic forms but simplified the architecture and made it more abstract. They also reimagined the palette. The result was a lightening and brightening, with white plaster walls, whitewashed log purloins, black steel windows, and a minimalist approach to furnishings. The great room is centered on the spectacular view of the Tetons.

The process began by reimagining the existing structure. "We had to retain the skeleton of the main house to accommodate the county overlay," explains Logan. "We simplified the architecture and made it more abstract. It is now three black gable forms with a separate little black box all knit together with a porch, a transition piece that links them all on the south side."

The structure's two primary gables, connected by a high roofline, house the common spaces, and, at the eastern end, the master bedroom suite. The third gabled form, which encompasses the guest quarters, is joined by a low peaked-roof connector that serves as the glass-walled entry and transition space between programs. To the west, a low flat roof creates a covered porch, punctuated in the middle, above a raised planter bed, leading to the garage. The newly elongated structure allows for a connected outdoor space in the form of an extended covered porch on the arrival side. On the view side, patio areas give way to the grassy landscape of the riverine meadow environment, where landscape architects at Hershberger Design oversaw creek reclamation, planted natural landscaping and created a footpath leading to a fire pit at creek's edge.

The exterior and interior palettes were also simplified and pared down: the logs were painted black and the roof was replaced with black standing-seam steel. Inside, white plaster walls contrast with blackish-blue Belgian stone floors and black steel detailing for a dramatically modern effect. The furnishings, a multi-person effort involving interior designers Lorraine Letendre at the outset and Elisa Chambers of Snake River Interiors at the conclusion, in collaboration with the owners and CLB, take a reductive approach. Furniture is minimal; floors are uniform throughout most of the house. The black-and-white theme is carried through into the kitchen, where whitewashed millwork contrasts with black countertops and minimalist hardware. The most striking elements are the house's patinated steel details: the stair railing, the leather-wrapped handrail, and the fireplace with its guillotine door, all handcrafted to CLB's specifications by Brandner Design in Bozeman, Montana.

What began as "a well-intentioned 'let's keep it simple' remodel," relates Logan, "to turn the house into something that felt more timeless. Like the Hans Christian Anderson story of the ugly duckling, it was a hastily put-together building that turned into something amazing," and given the Teton-view prospect over the swan ponds, seems entirely appropriate.

Black stained logs, black steel details, and black painted wood constitute a modern twist on the classic log cabin. The three gabled forms are oriented over open meadows toward live water and the mountain views. The steep pitch of the steel standing-seam roofs helps accumulated snow slide off in winter.

ABOVE LEFT: Interior design was a collaboration by the owners with designer Lorraine Letendre, Elisa Chambers of Snake River Interiors, and Jennifer Mei of CLB Architects. A quiet corner in a passageway, with a hair-on-hide rug and slipcovered chair, offers a light-bathed spot for reading.

ABOVE RIGHT AND FACING: The guillotine-door fireplace with steel surround, manufactured by Brandner Design, makes a refined modern statement in the great room.

ARCTICA
THE VA ISHING NORTH
Sebastian Copeland

THE WILD HORSES OF SABLE ISLAND
Roberto Dutesco

FACING: The heavily patinated steel staircase rail panel, by metal artisan Jeff Brandner of Brandner Design, makes a bold architectural statement in the living area and balances the fireplace on the opposite end. A simple block wood bench allows an unobstructed view to the mountains for diners seated in the tall chairs. Black-blue Belgian slate flooring extends throughout the open plan.

ABOVE: The kitchen is a study in contrast: black countertops and floors against white cabinets and plaster walls. The oak cabinets were wire-brushed and whitewashed. A collection of handmade vessels displayed near the ceiling draws the eye upward and adds an organic touch.

LEFT: The entry is both dramatic—with its entire wall of glass, oversized door, and exposed log ends—and restrained in its feeling of containment. The seamless transition between indoor and outdoor highlights the craftsmanship of site superintendent Gary Zundel and his team from Ankeny Construction Management.

ABOVE: The quiet bedroom is a study in tranquility, with neutral tones and natural fibers.

A black-and-white bathroom featuring limestone and marble opens directly onto a meadow, its glass doors offering a full on view of a rocky bluff that comes down to the edge of the property.

ABOVE TOP: Meticulous attention to detail is evident in Brandner's craftsmanship.

ABOVE AND RIGHT: The landscaping, in which the natural meadow comes right up to the edge of the house, was conceived by Hershberger Design. The long, low exterior covered walkway links the garage structure to the main house where it extends the length of the arrival side. An opening in the ceiling above a raised planter lightens the roof mass.